IN THE FIELD

IN THE FIELD

JOAN SULLIVAN

P.O. Box 2188, St. John's, NL, Canada, A1C 6E6
WWW.BREAKWATERBOOKS.COM

Copyright © 2012 Joan Sullivan
LIBRARY AND ARCHIVES CANADA CATALOGUING IN PUBLICATION
Sullivan, Joan, 1963-
In the field / Joan Sullivan.
Includes bibliographical references.
ISBN 978-1-55081-391-3
1. Norris, Stephen--Influence. 2. World War, 1914-1918--Casualties--
Newfoundland and Labrador--Three Arms. 3. World War, 1914-1918--
Social aspects--Newfoundland and Labrador--Three Arms.
4. Three Arms (N.L.)--History. I. Title.
FC2195.T57S85 2012   971.8   C2012-904976-X

Breakwater Books acknowledges the support of the Canada Council for the Arts, which last year invested $154 million to bring the arts to Canadians throughout the country.We acknowledge the Government of Canada through the Canada Book Fund and the Government of Newfoundland and Labrador through the Department of Tourism, Culture and Recreation for our publishing activities.

PRINTED AND BOUND IN CANADA.

Canada Council Conseil des Arts   Canadä   Newfoundland
for the Arts   du Canada   Labrador

CORPORAL WILLIAM SULLIVAN

OPENING NOTE

"Reportedly, the death of Stephen Norris in World War I left the Three Arms business without an heir apparent— the firm and the Norris family left the village after the death of James Norris in 1924."
– from *The Encyclopedia of Newfoundland and Labrador*[1]

❀

IT is a myth that Stephen Norris was the last surviving son. In fact, Stephen Norris was survived by three brothers, although none worked on Three Arms Island as they were busy with family business concerns elsewhere. But the idea that the loss of Stephen Norris left his family and his community bereft and heirless and, ultimately, extinguished took root and spread.[2]

But that was not the whole story.

And that was not the end of the story.

---

[1] The Encyclopedia of Newfoundland and Labrador, (St. John's: Harry Cuff Publications Ltd., 1994), 379.

[2] This and other information on Stephen Norris from an interview with and archival material provided by Bert Riggs, archivist with Memorial University's Archives and Special Collections, QEII Library. Any errors are the author's.

PROLOGUE

There blows a cold nor'wester

❀

TWO months after the initial fighting at Beaumont Hamel
fell into dead silence, a new and different note sounded in
the field. It was September 1916; Stephen Norris and the
rest of the Regiment were at the Ypres Salient in Belgium,
and "D" Company was hosting a party for the officers.
And someone was playing...the accordion. Someone was
playing..."The Banks of Newfoundland."

> ...and as the music came from the instrument the
> sandbagged walls of our 'H. Q.' seemed to fade. "The
> Banks of Newfoundland" rang in our ears, and we saw
> once more the tented slopes of Quidi Vidi on Regatta
> Day.[3]

The rain fell, and the shells. Harsh chill whispers, portent
whistles. But the notes played and played. So far from home,
from Newfoundland, they played and played.

---

[3] Officer's description, "Reveille," *Newfoundland Quarterly* 104.1 (2011),
61.

CHAPTER ONE

Only the Future Lies Ahead

❁

1892.

A leap year.

Ellis Island opens. Lizzie Borden's father and stepmother are found murdered in their home in Fall River, Massachusetts. Sir Arthur Conan Doyle publishes *The Adventures of Sherlock Holmes. The Nutcracker*, with music by Tchaikovsky, debuts in St. Petersburg. Grover Cleveland is elected President of the United States, and William Gladstone begins his fourth and final term as British Prime Minister. James Naismith introduces the rules of basketball, and Sir Frederick Stanley donates the Stanley Cup to Canadian hockey. Poet Walt Whitman and the coward Robert Ford die. Mary Pickford, J. R. R. Tolkien, and Haile Selassie are born.

In Newfoundland, almost all the commercial, domestic, and ecclesiastical architecture in St. John's is razed by The Great Fire, of July 8, with $13,000,000 in damages, 11,000 left homeless, but, astonishingly, only three lives lost. That same year, Sir William Whiteway is elected Prime Minister for the second time, retaining Liberal Party rule. Twenty-four landsmen sealers die in Trinity Bay, and Confederation negotiations between the self-governing colony and Canadian

Prime Minister, Sir John Thompson, almost come to fruition—an event for celebration or consternation, depending on your politics. And, throughout the city and in the outports of the harbours and bays all over Newfoundland, Stephen Norris and the other infants who will become the soldiers of WWI take their first breaths.

❀

THREE Arms Island is in northern Notre Dame Bay. Its length and width span a few miles. Schooners visited the island for fishing, and when people began staying permanently, they built their stages, flakes, and wharves on the beach running along the island's eastern side. Only a slender seawater channel, a tickle, divided the island from the shore.

The first settlers were two brothers, John and William Wells, and their families. The Wellses were from Twillingate and, before that, from Ringwood, England, which they left in 1792. They were followed by the Strongs (also of Ringwood) and various Coopers, Burts, Vincents, Batstones, Rowsells, and Bartletts, all English or descended from English settlers. Solomon Strong married Jane Wells, and John Wells in turn married Solomon's sister.[4]

The census of 1845 lists 29 people, all working in the fishery. The census of 1857 lists 58; of 1869, 69; of 1884, 102. Three Arms was growing.

As throughout Newfoundland, the economy revolved around the fishery, which was small-boat, inshore, and exceptionally

---

[4]   Solomon died in 1894, "after a short illness," aged 85; he was pre-deceased by his wife, Jane, who died in 1888, sadly, "after a long and painful illness." Obituaries from the *Twillingate Sun*. Private Collection of John Wheeler.

successful. In 1884, there was one merchant/trader on Three Arms, John Wells. John and William Wells built five schooners to exchange cargo in St. John's, including the *Royal George*, which caught fire with a complete loss of ship and cargo, but all crew saved; the *Sweet Home*, which John Wells loved despite its reputation as the worst vessel in Newfoundland waters; and a sailing ship christened *The Bulley*. Solomon Strong was the main boat builder, and he crafted small boats, trap skips, and a small schooner.

Parts of the island were cleared for growing vegetables, and there was one fulltime farmer, along with 49 fishermen (who also farmed subsistence). In 1891 there were 17 males and 20 females engaged in the small-scale summer fishery as well as animal husbandry and, in the spring, sealing. John Wells also started a sawmill.

At first, the children were educated by John Wells, who voluntarily taught his and Solomon Strong's offspring in the evenings. Then the Methodists paid a teacher's wages while the families contributed bread and board. When Roman Catholic families came, the two denominations supplied the teacher in turn and in accordance to which faith had the most children in attendance. In 1907, most were Methodist: Dimond, Curtis, English, Strathon, Swyers, Marsh, Strong, Moss. The Catholic family names included Morriarty, Fitzgerald, Deldbery, Butler, Burke, and Stapleton. Such cooperation was sensible and somewhat unique. There was an imbalance between the religions, but no strife; it seems everyone got along fine, worshipping at either the Methodist church on the mainland or the Catholic chapel on the island. The children also performed entertainments of dialogues ("Acting the Gossip"), recitations ("The Foolish Pair"), and songs ("Yankee Doodle") with set material, such as screens and a chandelier, borrowed from family homes.

Three Arms Island enjoyed plenty of contact, not just with

visitors from its own country, but from overseas. On Saturday nights the harbour gave shelter to schooners from all over Notre Dame Bay, and they anchored so closely together it was possible to cross from the island to the mainland via their decks. Everyone would gather at the store for storytelling, dancing, and a drink of dark rum. Some seamen came from very far away, and girls would fall in love, marry, and sail to a new home as remote and exotic as America, Wales, and New Zealand.

Three Arms was linked to the world. In the early 20th century there was a telegraph office, the first in the bay, operated by Nellie Moores for more than 20 years. The government eventually stationed the office in her house, to save her the commute (sometimes she had to row herself across the tickle). From here, men could send to worried families the message: "Harboured at Three Arms; All Well." This entailed a telegraph road from Middle Arm to Jackson's Cove and Silverdale, and in the winter this served to cart mail.

When John Wells retired, James Norris became the merchant and general dealer of Three Arms Island and the only merchant in northern Notre Dame Bay. He was named for his father, who had come from Waterford, Ireland, and married Catherine Dollard; they had first settled in Petty Harbour near St. John's where he was a planter.

James Norris started large-scale trading. He had branches all over White Bay. He held extensive mining interests along the coast and went to Nipper's Harbour for pit props (lumber to reinforce the tunnels). He commissioned big schooners, two dozen of them, including the *Mary*, a 40-tonner built by Con Lake; the *Irish Lass*; the *Rover's Bride*; and, in the year of Haley's comet, 1910, the 16-tonner the *Comet*. These were built by Charlie and Thomas King in Harry's Harbour and were also fitted with marine engines. They made seasonal trips down the Labrador and traded fish for freight in St. John's as well as exporting fish to Oporto, Portugal. James Norris's last boat was built in 1916, by Abraham Rideout, and named for his daughter, Nell.[5]

James Norris employed many men, and he also had young women working in his store and sometimes as his secretary. A devout Roman Catholic, he built the small chapel for his family. Before that, Mass was said in the Norris house when a priest made a rare visit—it could be years between services although the Lenten rosary and other rituals were observed.

James Norris and his wife, Mary Ann (née Dower, of Conche), had seven sons and one daughter. John (1879) was the eldest; his family and friends called him Jack. Next was Ambrose (1888). A third son, James (c. 1889), named for his father and grandfather, studied at St. Bonaventure's, worked in the family's businesses, "and was liked by everyone for his quiet inoffensive manner."[6] But he died in April, 1905, on Pentecost Sunday, at the General Hospital; he had been ill with some mysterious malady, but his death was still a shock. His parents were not with him, but his body was returned to Three Arms Island, his headstone inscribed "beloved son". Bernard (1890) also boarded at St. Bonaventure's.

[5] Nell, formally Ellen, also called Nelly, married William Jackman, a tailor from St. John's, in the chapel on Three Arms in 1907. "United hand and heart," read a contemporary report, "The very popular and accomplished Miss Nelly Norris was elegantly costumed in white satin, with regulation veil and orange blossoms. The honeymoon is being spent at Three Arms. The groom's present to the bride was a gold crescent brooch, with rubies and pearls, and to the (3) bridesmaids, diamond rings." They had 12 children, spent many years living on Mundy Pond Road in St. John's, and eventually moved to Montreal.

[6] *The Adelphian*, 1905.

Stephen Casimir[7] Norris was born in 1892.

There followed William, born in 1895, who died of pneumonia in July 1906, and Walter, born in 1899, who died April 13, 1903, possibly of diphtheria. Nell (1884), formally Ellen, was the only girl.

Thus, at the outbreak of hostilities in 1914, Stephen Norris was the youngest of the four remaining sons in the family. And, legend tells, it was Stephen Norris who carried the future of Three Arms Island into the First World War.

THE NORRIS FAMILY IN 1923. Back row, left to right: Bernard, John, Ambrose, and Ellen. Seated: James and Mary. INSET: Stephen Norris in his regiment uniform.

7   St. Casimir (1458–1484) was a prince in the Kingdom of Poland and is the patron saint of Poland, Lithuania, and the young.

CHAPTER TWO

The Call to Arms

❀

ON June 28, 1914, Archduke Franz Ferdinand of Austria and his wife, Sophie, Duchess of Hohenberg, were assassinated in Sarajevo by Gavrilo Princip, a Bosnian Serb and a member of the nationalist Black Hand society. It was 'the shot heard round the world' though Princip actually fired twice. At first, the slaying of the Austro-Hungarian heir appeared a cruel but far-off incident, yet it wasn't long before the bullet's trajectory encircled the globe. In just 37 days, the world was at war.[8]

Austria-Hungary saw an opening to move against the Serbs, the Germans an opportunity to extend their influence, and the powers in London, Paris, and St. Petersburg the need to immediately check both advances. Thus the Allies—England, France, Belgium, Russia, and Serbia, and eventually Italy and the United States—stood against the Central Powers of Germany, Austria-Hungary, the Turkish forces, and Bulgaria. The gun Princip fired was the ignition point for The War to End All Wars. Before it was over, four empires—Austria-Hungary, Imperial Germany, Ottoman Turkey, and Tsarist Russia—would be erased.

---

[8] Ian F. W. Beckett, *The Great War* 1914-1918. 2nd ed. (Harlow: Pearson Education Limited, 2007), 22.

At midnight on August 4, 1914, Britain, on behalf of the Empire, declared war against Germany. Newfoundland, a British Dominion, now entered the fray.[9]

The Newfoundland government, then headed by Sir Edward Morris[10] and his People's Party, didn't have a military department or any money to finance one. "From a military standpoint no country could be in a state of greater unpreparedness."[11] Still, Britain had called for soldiers and sacrifice. Newfoundland would answer.

Newfoundland's connection to Britain was not ancient history. It was a source of living pride. The Newfoundlanders held fast to their identity. They were not Canadian—not American. They were fighting for their flag, their King, and Mother England. They did not want to hear "The Maple Leaf" from welcoming bands, but "The Banks of Newfoundland."[12]

Newfoundland raised its own war loan of $6 million. The Newfoundland Patriotic Association (NPA), a non-partisan group that quickly counted 300 members, was founded to

---

[9]   As did Australia, Canada, New Zealand, and South Africa. Ibid. 89.

[10] Photos show Morris with thick, distinguished, graying side-parted hair and a prominent moustache styled like an inverted 'V,' a popular fashion at the time. Before WWI ended, Morris would invite the Official Opposition to join the Government, an unusual move even in a time noted for shifting political dalliances. But Morris felt Newfoundland needed a government supported by all parts of the island, and both Catholic and Protestant religions. Towards the end of the war Morris received a peerage, the title of Baron, and moved to London where he sat in the House of Lords. He died in London in 1935.

[11] Richard Cramm, *The First Five Hundred, Being a historical sketch of the military operations of the Royal Newfoundland Regiment in Gallipoli and on the Western Front during the Great War (1914-1918)* (New York: C. F. Williams and Son Inc.), 19.

[12] Francis T. Lind, *The Letters of Mayo Lind, Newfoundland's Unofficial War Correspondent 1914-1916* (St. John's: Robinson & Co., Limited, 1919; St. John's: Creative Book Publishing, 2001), 3. Citations refer to the Creative Book Publishing edition.

recruit and train 500 soldiers.

About 12,000 men would try to enlist—15.3% of the male population of Newfoundland. 6,241 joined the Regiment, and a near equal number, 6,184, volunteered and were rejected.[13] They were recruited into the three Newfoundland forces: the Newfoundland Regiment, the Royal Naval Reserve, and the Newfoundland Forestry Corps. Newfoundlanders also served with the Canadian Expeditionary Force and the Merchant Marine.

The First Five Hundred (actually 537), the 'Blue Puttees'— named for their blue, instead of the usual (unavailable) khaki broadcloth bands that wrapped the tops of their boots—sailed on October 4, 1914. They were a land force although William F. Coaker, the fiery Fishermen's Protective Union leader who'd been elected in 1913 to the General Assembly, favoured the Navy because it was felt the war would be fought and won on land, not at sea. They formed "A" and "B" Companies of the Regiment's 1st Battalion. They would receive further training at Salisbury Plain in England, Fort George, Stobs Camp, and Ayr in Scotland.

The Newfoundland Regiment was assigned to the 88th Brigade of the 29th Division,[14] an infantry division of the British Army. 6,241 Newfoundlanders would join the Regiment; only Newfoundlanders could sign up.[15]

---

[13] Richard Hibbs, ed. *Who's Who in and from Newfoundland, 1927* (St. John's: 1927), 43.

[14] A Regiment, commanded by a Colonel, contains between 1000 and 3000 soldiers; a Brigade, commanded by a Brigadier, contains two regiments; and a Division, usually commanded by a Major General, contains several brigades.

[15] This was more descriptive than restrictive and was flexible enough to allow able-bodied young men from other countries who were working in Newfoundland to join the Regiment. Ultimately, the Regiment included a minority of soldiers from many nations, including Canada, France, and Russia.

Patriotic response and fervour was strongest in the capital city of St. John's. For one thing, Morris and the People's Party were supported by the Roman Catholics who dominated, by population and therefore mercantile and political influence, St. John's and most of the Avalon Peninsula, while much of the rest of Newfoundland was Protestant. More importantly, the outports had their own economic concerns. On Three Arms Island, as throughout outharbour Newfoundland, the demand for fish-industry labour was intense. The market was always vulnerable to exterior forces, and now the price for fish was rising.

Still, the war was not expected to last long. The British Government informed its troops they would be home by Christmas. Expectations of victory were high, fuelled by patriotism and loyalty to the Crown: "Huge Crowds Cheer Their Majesties at Palace," noted British headlines. Men rushed to join up so as not to miss their chance to participate. The best educated were the most enthusiastic to do their bit. The popular English poet Rupert Brooke was not alone when he heralded the coming adventure as something enviable, gallant, and fine.

THE DEAD

Blow out, you bugles, over the rich Dead!
There's none of these so lonely and poor of old,
But, dying, has made us rarer gifts than gold.
These laid the world away; poured out the red
Sweet wine of youth; gave up the years to be

Of work and joy, and that unhoped serene,
That men call age; and those who would have been,
Their sons, they gave, their immortality.

Blow, bugles, blow! They brought us, for our dearth,
Holiness, lacked so long, and Love, and Pain.
Honour has come back, as a king, to earth,

And has paid his subjects with a royal wage;
And Nobleness walks in our ways again;
And we have come into our heritage.

— BY RUPERT BROOKE[16]

The first physical requirements for volunteers were that they be aged 18 to 35 and at least 5 feet 4 inches, 140 lbs, with a chest expansion of 35 inches. Anyone from outside of St. John's who wanted to volunteer went to the local magistrate, who gave him a free ticket to the city. Most volunteers came in late winter or early spring. The drill training, which at first paid nothing, was soon offering $1 a day, for some a rare opportunity to earn a cash wage. The first volunteers were taken "for the duration—but not more than one year."[17] They would need to re-enlist while still training in England.

The initial prediction that the war would be over quickly, the troops home by Christmas, had been superseded by technology. The modern war machine had incredible capacity, range, accuracy, and rate of fire. Since the 1890s, quick-firing artillery and machine guns had been used. There were submarines and mines and torpedoes. But the European military elite disdained such apparatus. It was only two years since the unsinkable *Titanic* had sunk; what could progress promise that the traditional bayonet, sabre, and lance, let alone the ideals of honour and glory, not fulfill?[18]

---

[16] Rupert Brooke, *Rupert Brooke: The Collected Poems*, (London: Sidgwick & Jackson, 1987), 314. Rupert Brooke (1887-1915) was a popular English poet who served with the Royal Navy and died of sepsis en route to Gallipoli.

[17] Gerald W. L. Nicholson, *The Fighting Newfoundlander: A History of The Royal Newfoundland Regiment* (Montreal: McGill-Queen's University Press, 2006), 106.

[18] Beckett, *The Great War*, 55.

Such beliefs paralleled the propaganda surrounding the war, which was extreme. Both sides had their atrocity stories. The Germans bayoneted babies and had tied the monks in Antwerp to their abbey's bells, torturing them to death. The French poisoned German wells with plague and blinded German prisoners of war. Posters portrayed the Germans as skeletons drinking goblets of blood. British newspapers claimed the Germans had crucified a Canadian soldier. At the same time, news sources on either side were severely restricted on what they could report from the front lines, including troop movements and casualties.

STEPHEN NORRIS

Whatever the headlines shouted, the war had not ended by Christmas. More soldiers were needed.

In 1915, there was a drive for a 2nd Battalion. The Patriotic Association urged outport men to enlist now and worry about the economy later. But the young outport men *were* the economy, its muscular engine, in the inshore fishery, the Labrador fishery, the seal hunt, and all other aspects of household production. "They were engrossed in a means of livelihood that could not be put off for a month, or even a week, but a kind of work upon the success of one brief week of which the happiness of the family for the entire year might depend."[19]

The physical requirements were deemed too exclusive and a wider net was cast. In March 1915, the standards were dropped to 18 years, 5 feet tall, and 112 lbs. There were 43 physical reasons for rejection ('poor physique,' 'pleurisy,' 'fits,' 'drunk'), and the men were categorized from Class A, Fit for General Service, to Class E, Unfit for Service.[20] Conscription, a contentious policy, was introduced in 1918, but no conscripts served as the war ended while they were still in training.

Stephen Norris had attended St. Bonaventure's from 1908 to 1911, and after graduation he worked in his father's business for four years before joining the Regiment's 2nd Battalion.

---

[19] Cramm, *The First Five Hundred*, 19.

[20] "When you are asked by your children, in the years to come, what part you took in the Great War, will your answer be that you played a man's part, or that you played the part of a coward and a slacker. Your duty lies straight before you. Enlist at once. Go to the nearest Magistrate or Justice of the Peace, or other reputable person, and voluntarily offer your services. All your expenses will be paid to St. John's, and, if accepted, you will be immediately clothed in the King's Uniform. You will be paid one dollar and ten cents ($1.10) per day, with an allowance of ninety cents (90 cents) for maintenance while in Newfoundland. After you leave here your maintenance will be looked after in addition to your pay." Captain Rev. Thomas Nangle, *The Trail of the Caribou* (St. John's: 1918).

He enlisted January 9, 1915, in St. John's. He was one of a group of about 50; about 118 men volunteered each month that year. In his papers, under the heading "Special Reserve," the handwritten information attested that he had been examined on January 4, 1915, in St. John's: he was 22; his trade, Assistant Manager, General Merchant; he was 5 feet 7 inches tall; his chest measured 38½ inches; and he had been vaccinated in 1910. His regimental number was 921.

On February 24, 1915, he was promoted from Private to Corporal. He had a real knack for training men.

On April 13, 1915, he was transferred to "C" Company. On July 12, 1915, he was appointed to Second Lieutenant, with Seniority. "Second Lieutenant Stephen C. Norris is a son of James Norris, Esq., Merchant, of Three Arms, Green Bay," read a contemporary article, in the *Newfoundland Quarterly*.

> After a successful career at St. Bonaventure's College he entered into his father's business and was actively engaged therein when the call for volunteers came and he enlisted as a private. Showing special aptitude for the training of men he was promoted to Sergeant and retained at St. John's to assist in this work, and his excellent services later won him a Lieutenancy, to which we feel sure he will do justice. [21]

And the men liked him; they gave him a present when he was transferred.

On October 27, 1915, when Stephen Norris left on the train from St. John's to travel by rail and boat to Quebec, he and another Catholic officer, Lieutenant Kevin Keegan, were not

---

[21] "New Lieutenants – Newfoundland Regiment," *Newfoundland Quarterly* 15.3 (1916), 4.

given first-class seats (just a baggage car, not a sleeper) on the train, as the Protestant officers had been. James Norris was upset at this disparity and offered to buy first-class seats, in fact the entire first-class coach, as a remedy.[22]

"C" Company (more than three quarters of the enlisted men from the outports) was the last full Company to go overseas in 1915 as a single draft. The company left St. John's under the command of Captain Alexander Montgomerie and from Quebec sailed on the H. M. T. *Corsican*, disembarking at Devonport on November 9, 1915, and then traveling to military camp at Gailes, 12 miles from Ayr. There they were quartered in huts, in a military camp, as there was no room at the Regimental Depot.[23]

---

[22] This story has come down through the Norris family; the ultimate resolution of the issue is not known.

[23] The Depot was a military hub where Battalions were attached to larger Divisions before embarking to Gallipoli or the Western Front.

CHAPTER THREE

The Machine of War

❁

THE war that Stephen Norris dutifully volunteered for was different than any previous armed conflict. Much of the technology that ignited, cloaked, enlarged, and sustained it had never been seen before.[24] But the soldiers were still flesh and bone.

On January 19, 1915, German zeppelins began their night raids in British skies, approaching within and above the clouds. Zeppelins were named after their designer, Count Ferdinand von Zeppelin, who first conceived of them in 1874. He had been intrigued with the French military's method of using balloons for mail delivery during the Franco-Prussian War of 1870-1871. Von Zeppelin patented his invention in 1899.

Before WWI, zeppelins were employed in commercial travel, but when the fighting started, their use shifted to reconnaissance and, later, bombing raids. They were part of both the German Army and Navy.

In September 1915, the first trenches were dug on the Western front. From these, the soldiers faced the introduction

---

[24] Much of the information on the military tactics and weaponry of WWI was provided by an interview with Dr. Mike O'Brien, Department of History, Memorial University of Newfoundland. Any errors are the author's.

of many new tactics and weapons, including flame-throwers, gas, and the widespread use of machine guns.

The first tanks were used on the Somme in August, 1916. The British first deployed these caterpillar-treaded, machine-gun-turreted weapons; indeed (as we shall see) they had invented them.

Submarines, or German U-boats, were launched with the start of the war. They had first been used in the American War of Independence (1775-1783). But none of those submarines operated successfully. The Confederate sub *H. L. Hunley* in the American Civil War (1861-1865) did sink a Union ship, but its own lifespan was brief and trouble-ridden.

It was about 1875 when John Philip Holland, an Irish engineer, was asked by the Fenian Society to design a submarine (the Fenians were the American branch of the 19th century Irish Republican Brotherhood; Holland's brother was a member). He developed the dual-propulsion submarine with a diesel engine to run on the surface and an electric motor to run underwater. *Fenian Ram* was tested in 1881. Soon after, Holland and the Society quarrelled and parted ways, but in 1895 he was contracted as a designer with the U. S. Navy. In 1898 the successful *Holland* was launched. Orders soon came in from England and Russia.

These were the submarines used for the first time in the First World War, and very effectively.

The German submarine strategy has received more attention than the Allies' because the British and French provided more targets. The British and French navies were active and vulnerable while the German warships stayed fairly close to home. The German submarine U-20 also notoriously torpedoed and sank the RMS *Lusitania* on May 7, 1915; what had once been the largest ship in the world sank in twenty minutes with 1,195 of 1,959 passengers and crew lost. The

Allies said *Lusitania* was a passenger liner while the Germans insisted that the ship was a legitimate military objective, and the controversy continues still.

What really extended the war's destructive reach was the use of airplanes. Airplanes were first used in a small war between Italy and the Ottoman Empire in Libya in 1911-1912. An Italian pilot dropped four handheld bombs on Turkish soldiers. WWI was the first time airplanes were used in very large numbers by both sides.

These were fixed-wing "aeroplanes" of hardwood, steel wire, and linen. They debuted as agents of reconnaissance, but air combat soon followed. In the first engagements, the pilots threw bricks at each other or rope—which they hoped would become tangled in the propellers. Then they fired hand-held firearms. When all else failed, the pilots rammed the enemy plane. More sophisticated maneuvers, and mounted machine guns, did follow. The exploits seemed daredevil, and pilots from both sides were regarded as knights, heroes who rode the sky.

At the same time, for much of the war, ground action was entrenched. Excepting the movements of the first month and the last year, when trenches finally could not stop advances anymore, the enemy was often no more than a few yards away, the soldiers often able to communicate with each other through shouting or crude signs. For example, in June 1916, Field Marshall Horatio Herbert Kitchener, the British Secretary of State for War, a polarizing figure and one of the few at that level of British command who foresaw a lengthy conflict, drowned when his ship the H. M. S. *Hampshire* was torpedoed and sunk. The Germans hoisted a mocking message of condolence: "We sympathize with you in the loss of Kitchener," which the Newfoundlanders read. In fact, this was the means by which they first learned what happened.[25]

Such proximity meant chemical warfare could be conducted

via grenades although delivery by shells was more usual. The Germans used gas first, at Ypres in 1915. Within weeks, the British and French used it as well. They had all been developing chemical weapons—WWI was sometimes called "the chemist's war"—but nobody wanted to be the first to use them (or even call it "gas" as "accessories" was the common euphemism).[26] But as soon as the Germans did—and the British and French governments quickly denounced them for using illegal weapons—within a couple of weeks, the Allies were unleashing the same poisons themselves. From then on, gas was a constant. The chemicals included tear gas, chlorine, and phosgene.

For the soldiers in the trenches, it was the worst thing they endured. Although ultimately not effective in terms of determining any battle, the gas attacks were awful. When the first clouds of gas appeared, panicked soldiers simply fled. Then they were advised to protect their breathing with cotton pads, dipped in a solution of bicarbonate of soda, or urine-drenched cloth.[27] In 1915, Newfoundlander Dr. Cluny Macpherson invented the gas mask, fashioning it from metal and fabric. After that, gas attacks were rarely fatal. But they made life miserable for the soldiers. And it grew worse as the war continued, especially in 1917 with the deployment of mustard gas, which killed few soldiers but created big, horrible blisters.

Under the sea, above the clouds. Dug into the earth, borne on the air. The Great War was now Total War, "Der Totale Krieg"; German Chief of Staff, Erich Ludendorff, was the first to use the term, in 1919.[28]

---

[25]   Lind, *The Letters of Mayo Lind*, 139-140.

[26]   "Weapons of War," last modified August 22, 2009, http://www.firstworldwar.com/weaponry/gas.htm

[27]   Ibid.

[28]   Beckett, *The Great War*, 344.

CHAPTER FOUR

Entrenched in the Dardanelles: "The heat, the hard work, the flies…"

❀

STEPHEN Norris and all the other Newfoundland soldiers had enlisted with the idea they would soon find themselves fighting in France, delivering a well-deserved lesson to the Germans. But their arc from embarkation in St. John's to deployment on the frontlines had a long and unexpected trajectory. The First Five Hundred, "A" and "B" Companies,[29] who had sailed on the *Florizel*, found themselves on Salisbury Plain, in the southern part of England, where they stayed for October, November, and December 1914. Then they moved up to Scotland, first at Fort George, and then, in February, to Edinburgh Castle. This is when "C" Company arrived but without Stephen Norris, who was retained in St. John's, training volunteers. It was also while they were in Edinburgh that they developed a relationship with the Royal Scots Regiment, one that has lasted; they were the only non-Scottish regiment to garrison at Edinburgh Castle.

In March and in May, "D" Company and "E" Company, respectively, sailed across. In May, they transferred to Stobs Camp on the Scottish border, and in July, "F" Company

---

[29] A "Company" includes up to 250 soldiers.

arrived, which increased the total to six companies and about 1500 soldiers.

For all this time, they were in training.

They moved to Ayr in the south-west of Scotland, which became their headquarters for most of the remainder of the war. In early August, they shifted to Aldershot, south of London, for 17 days. Here there were all kinds of formal ceremonies; and the Regiment soldiers marched and stood at attention as they were reviewed by Lord Kitchener and by King George V.

In 1917, King George V would reward the Regiment with the title "Royal" in recognition of their heart and courage, perhaps displayed most famously on the first day of the Somme Offensive on July 1, 1916. Historically known as the Battle of the Somme, at the time it was called the Allied Push, or The July Drive, which continued on into October.

❁

WHEN the 1st Battalion of the Newfoundland Regiment initially arrived in Europe and was assigned to the 88th Infantry Brigade, the soldiers found their time at Stobs Camp seemed interminable. It was as if they were forgotten by the Powers That Be, and they joked that years after the conflict ended they would still languish in training, an unchecked item on a lost memo. But events were moving.

On August 20, 1915, the 1076 men of the Newfoundland Regiment, of which 34 were officers, departed from Devonport on the HMS *Megantic*. Sailing the Mediterranean was uneventful, even restful. They landed on September 1 in Alexandria, Egypt.

There, in North Africa, they reinforced a division of British regular troops (as opposed to volunteers like themselves). Everyone around them was a professional soldier, and at first these professionals didn't like having the Newfoundlanders there. The British called the Newfoundlanders "The Five Bobbers," a reference to their payment of five shillings a day as opposed to the two shillings the British soldiers received. To the British, the Newfoundlanders were unseasoned and overpaid. That assessment would change.

After some militaristic bureaucratic back and forth, parading and inspection, and enduring swarms of flies, the Regiment boarded the *Prince Abbas* and, on September 20, sailed to Suvla Bay, carried ashore by specially reinforced motorboats.

This was Gallipoli, the Dardanelles Campaign. The goal was to capture Constantinople and establish a clear sea passage to Russia. Like much of the Allied strategy, the Dardanelles Campaign was supposed to end quickly—a swift, surprising, and effective offensive maneuver—but the fighting, which had started on April 15, had already lasted five months.

The Regiment's next three months were spent in dugouts and gullies. Water rations were a half a pint each day. On the first morning, the Regiment had its first casualty when Turkish shrapnel injured Captain Walter Rendell, who was evacuated and replaced by Captain Arthur (Tim) Raley. In late September, the Regiment lost its first soldier, Private Hugh McWhirter #902 of Humbermouth, Bay of Islands, and buried him on Hill 10.

Life in the trenches was hazardous, full of peril and vermin, and, hand-in-hand with all its potential dangers, quite tedious.

"The soldiers had come expecting to find war a life of excitement. They found it, on the contrary, duller than the most dreary spells of life in the back woods of their own island."[30] Their routine was framed by quotidian torment: "The heat, the hard work, the flies...."[31]

---

[30] Cramm, *The First Five Hundred*, 37.
[31] Ibid.

As one soldier, Lewis Bartlett, wrote, "It's very lonely here still troops are coming all the time & we do have to do quite a lot of transport work."[32]

Shells came from the Turkish side daily, and sniping was a constant threat and a lethal hazard when searching for water. A bullet could injure or kill any careless or unlucky soldier. But sickness and thirst were the real problems and quickly sapped the ranks. At first, the Regiment was divided in two, each half spelling the other after six or seven days on the front lines. But within weeks, the Regiment was so diminished by illness and dehydration they were all-in together and could no longer organize their own relief. Fortunately, they also found valuable comrades. In particular, the Australians, New Zealanders, and Newfoundlanders respected each other and fraternized well; the "Antipodean chums" shared their packages from home with the Regiment, whose own much-anticipated shipments of clothing and foodstuffs were taking ages to reach them.[33]

High opinion was earned. There were many instances of drama and heroism.

For example, after a raid on enemy snipers, Lieut. James Donnelly, of St. John's, who had attended St. Bonaventure's College with Stephen Norris and was his friend, was awarded the Military Cross due to the exemplary courage and skill demonstrated by Donnelly's patrol. The small party, aided by a few reinforcements, managed through fast, concentrated gunfire to hold off several times their number of Turkish soldiers, and in acknowledgement, the ridge they captured was renamed Caribou Hill.

---

[32] David R. Facey-Crowther, "The Soldier's Tale: Newfoundland Soldiers' Accounts of The Great War," (Talk to the Newfoundland Genealogical Society, November 23, 1999), 8.

[33] J. Alex Robinson, 1919 introduction to *The Letters of Mayo Lind*, by Francis T. Lind (St. John's: Creative Book Publishing, 2001), xxi.

Despite these combat engagements with the Turks, dubbed collectively "Abdul" by the British, the Turkish forces were not regarded as harshly as the German soldiers. The attitude of the Allies was that the Germans were forcing the Turks to fight. If the Newfoundlanders captured a Turk, they would give him water and food, especially a treat like apricot jam—the Turks, like all the soldiers, went long periods without anything sweet. The Turkish trenches were no better than the Newfoundlanders' and all the soldiers endured the same atrocious conditions. Lice were endemic, a misery, and the flies so thick on food it was hard to eat. Any foodstuff exposed was immediately crawling with vermin, even before they could get it to their mouths, and their clothing was continuously infested with lice.

Adding to the misery, the weather was the worst the Gallipoli peninsula had seen in 40 years. A ferocious thunderstorm lasted on and off for three weeks. Trenches were flooded waist-high. The drenchings created the threat of drowning on what had been parched land. They were followed directly by a drop in temperatures and the deluged trenches were frozen.

The Regiment soldiers had no overcoats. Trench foot swelled their feet so they could not wear boots; they wrapped them in sandbags stuffed with straw. Their toes became frostbitten.

Some of the soldiers were sealers, and the weather and circumstances were so bad it reminded them of the *Greenland* Disaster.[34] But they all survived the awful storm.

By December 20, in coincidence to their arrival date three months before, they were evacuating. Most left quickly, but remnants of the Regiment were present on that front into January.

There are 43 Newfoundlanders buried in Gallipoli.

❁

STEPHEN Norris was not at the Dardanelles, but kept back at Ayr for training. Having enlisted as a Private, he was moving up the ranks. Norris would have held legitimate promise for promotion—his education, his social standing. But officers needed to be replaced often because they were known to be target practice for the enemy.

Most of them were quickly slain on the field, partly because, in the early days of fighting, it was so easy to recognize an officer. While the regular soldiers were in khaki with puttees and a tin helmet, the officers went over the top in their leather boots up to their knees, their Sam Brown belt, their regular hat, and a pistol in their hand. So the Germans would fire at the officer because their loss left nobody in charge.[35] After a while, the British realized the benefits of outfitting the officers like the enlisted men.

[34] Cramm, *The First Five Hundred*, 51. In 1898 the S. S. Greenland lost 25 of 154 sealers in a ferociously cruel March storm.

[35] Riggs, interview.

TELEPHONE:- 8901 GERRARD (6 LINES).
TELEGRAMS:- "VICTORIOLA, WESTRAND, LONDON".

HÔTEL VICTORIA

LONDON

W.C.

Dec 12th 15

My Dear Moll,

I suppose this will be the last letter you will get from me for some time, as before I get the chance to write again, the "Prospero" will have finished.

As you will see by above I am at London, I came up for a course in Bombing that is to learn how to chuck

With the Draft about to leave
for the Dardanelles now.
I have no idea when
I will be going. I have been having
quite a nice time since
I came over, that is very
quick you know.
I have very interesting
things to tell you, so
I must go.
        Love to Kid
Jack & Self
            from
                Steve

Happy New Year to
everyone.

Hotel Victoria
London
W. C.
Dec 12th 15

My Dear Moll,[36]

I suppose this will be the last letter you will get from me for some time as before I get the chance to write again the "Prospero"[37] *will have finished.*

As you will see by above I am at London, I came up for a course in Bombing that is to learn how to chuck Bombs and to learn how they are made. I will be here a week then I go back to Ayr. I have not seen much of London, only came in this morning. However I am leading the simple life, so there will no cause for worry. It is about 6 weeks since we left St. John's, and I have not received any letters from home on French Shore.

Did you go south this fall or did you not. I suppose Jack [his brother John] is in St. John's about now. I should be very glad to hear from you or Jack and you can take it from me, I am fonder of both of you than either of you think. However I shall be expecting to hear from you very soon.

How is Fr Thibault[38] *I must write him soon.*

I suppose everything is about the same as usual and always will be on the French Shore, give my best regards to everyone. Leo Fitzpatrick is going with the Draft about to leave for the Dardanelles now. I have no idea when I will be going. I have been having quite a nice time since I came over that is very quick you know.

I have very interesting things to tell you, so I must go[?].

Love to kids Jack & self,

From

Steve [underlined]

Happy New Year to everyone.

---

[36] A nickname for Mary J. Stapleton, Stephen's sister-in-law, John (Jack)'s wife.

[37] The S. S. *Prospero* coastal boat was one of the Bowering Brothers' Fleet.

[38] The Rev. George Abner Thibault was Pastor of Conche Parish, appointed June 15, 1907. Hibbs, *Who's Who*, 187.

CHAPTER FIVE

What Isn't Said, What Isn't There to be Seen

❁

FIGHTING continued in the Dardanelles until the Allies withdrew on December 28. They had made no significant advances, and the sea route to Russia was not achieved. The Gallipoli campaign was a failure.[39]

But the Regiment had begun to earn its respect and reputation.

❁

IN mid-January, 1916, the Regiment was at Alexandria and about to fall in for Suez where they were encamped for several weeks. They were commanded by Lieutenant-Colonel A. L. Hadow, who was so British the soldiers joked he "slept at attention."[40] Hadow still held the initial British opinion that

---

[39] But for the Turks, it was a triumph that would lead to their independence. Turkey's first President, Mustafa Kemal Attaturk, was a commander with the successful Turkish forces at Dardanelles. He also made this famous tribute to the fallen: "You the mothers who sent their sons from far away countries, wipe away your tears, your sons are now lying in our bosom and are in peace. After having lost their lives on this land they are our sons as well." Kevin Fewster, Veciji Başarm, and Hatice Hürmüz Başarm, *Gallipoli: The Turkish Story* (Crows Nest, Australia: Allen and Unwin, 2003), 2.

[40] David Macfarlane, *The Danger Tree: Memory, War, and the Search for a Family's Past,* (Toronto: Macfarlane Walter & Ross, 1991), 60.

the Newfoundlanders were novices, untested on a battlefield. This despite their coming through Gallipoli with much strength and little loss and in an environment that was not actually the worst some of them had seen.

"We are the only battalion not regulars in the 29th Division," Rupert Bartlett wrote from Suez on January 25, 1916. "I think there's one territorial but not sure. Anyway we are as good as any of them, and can double the other regiments work anytime. Still it's an honour."[41]

They were in Suez for two months, and Hadow was very strict and put them through their paces. He did not see the Newfoundlanders had any training to equal that of the 29th Division. He also had some misgivings over the independent manner of the Newfoundland soldiers. In his opinion, it could be filed under laxity, inattention, even disobedience. Efficiency and discipline were paramount, and he set about instilling these virtues. Some of the Regiment were a bit disgruntled at Hadow's straight-laced austerity, but they would come to see the value of it once they journeyed to France. They also learned, and enjoyed, this song:

> I'm Hadow, some lad-o
> Just off the Staff
> I command the Newfoundlanders
> And they know it—not half;
> I'll make them or break them,
> I'll make the blighters sweat.
> For I'm Hadow, some lad-o,
> I'll be a General yet.

Hadow, the soldiers conceded, "made the Regiment."[42] The

---

[41]   Facey-Crowther, "The Soldier's Tale," 8.

[42]   Joy B. Cave, *What Became of Corporal Pittman?* (St. John': Breakwater Books, 1976), 62. In turn, Hadow would later tell CBC Radio the Newfoundland Regiment was "very magnificent material, young, inexperienced, but out to learn which they did." Quoted in Facey-Crowther, "The Soldier's Tale," 11.

training was useful; it would tell. The soldiers spent their time drilling, making 'Battalion Route Marches' of 14 miles through sand dunes, taking bombing courses, enjoying scheduled periods of 'Practical Rest,' waiting for the mail and parcels of books, clothing, and eatables that were chasing them from camp to post to front, and hearing rumours of the coming Push.

❀

THE Newfoundland Regiment sailed for Europe in March, reaching the port of Marseilles early in the morning of March 22.

Finally, France. This was where they had expected to be when they first enlisted. They could see that much had happened. In their letters home, which were censored, they noted:

> The women were doing the men's work; they were the
> ones ploughing the fields.
> There were old men.
> There were boys.
> There were young men on crutches, in bandages.
> But there were no fit young men.
> The women were wearing black.

The soldiers joked with each other, to keep their spirits up— gallows humour. That the war would end quickly was still the official line, but the rank and file no longer believed it. For example, a much-repeated circulating jest promised that Kitchener said the war would be over within the year—"but he didn't say WHAT year!"[43] They had some leave in England that spring, roughly eight days in London.

---

[43] Lind, *The Letters of Mayo Lind*, 121.

"Saw the best show in town," Regiment soldier H. G. R. Mews wrote. "Orchestra and chorus were great…judging by the people there one would never know there was a war on. London is a marvellous place if money was plentiful and would be worthwhile staying there."[44]

On Easter Eve, April 22, the Regiment, still part of the 88th Brigade, was back in the firing line. But the weather over France was bad, delaying the offensive.

They waited.

They wrote letters, sieved through the censors, shined their buttons, listened for "lights out." They practiced "pulling through" a rifle at the crack of dawn until the barrel glowed on the inside like a new shilling. They asked each other, "Has Reveille gone yet?"[45]

They ate bully beef (corned beef, army rations) and apricot jam.

They went to the cinema and watched Charlie Chaplin films, released as frequently as weekly by Keystone Studios: *The Flirts, Charlie at the Studio, Down and Out*. Chaplin was very popular with the soldiers. They thought him the finest comic they had ever seen. They retuned a popular song with the lyrics:

> Oh the moon shines bright on Charlie Chaplin,
> His boots are crackin'
> For the want of blackin'
> And his baggy trousers want mendin'
> Before they send him to the Dardanelles.[46]

---

[44] H. G. R. Mews, quoted in Facey-Crowther, "The Soldier's Tale," 7.
[45] Lind, *The Letters of Mayo Lind*, 121.
[46] Ibid.

Like all soldiers, they had their own vernacular, what the French called "l'argot des tranchees," the slang of the trenches, a vocabulary of war. Butter was "axle grease," an army chaplain "a devil dodger," an Italian solider "macaroni," a cemetery "a rest camp." There was even a slang term for using slang terms: "to sling the bat."

The Germans were "alleyman" or "boche"—a French term that originally meant something like "rascal" or "obstinate person"—or, more commonly, "Fritz," a nickname (as the British were "Tommies"). The Germans, in turn, called to the Newfoundlanders, "Hullo, red men," knowing that Newfoundland was once inhabited by the Beothuk who adorned their bodies with red ochre. Later they called the Regiment soldiers "White Indians from Newfoundland."[47]

They put these and other texts up over their trenches for the Newfoundland soldiers to read, such as the message conveying Kitchener's death.

The Allied soldiers held impromptu concerts, nicknaming their own comedians after the best: Chaplin. Crown and Anchor was a popular betting game. They played football (soccer) matches and other competitive sports. There was talk of sending a hockey team to Paris. Their days could have moments that were oddly domestic:

> Newfoundlanders are home lads first and last. They know when it is time for the squid to be in on the jigging grounds, and when the caplin ought to be rolling on the beach. They talk about the herring catch

---

[47] Lind, *The Letters of Mayo Lind*, 136-139. Germans had a long fascination with North American aboriginals. Karl Friedrich May (1842-1912), one of the most popular German writers ever, introduced "natives" into the German public's romantic imagination with his best-selling tales of Old West adventure.

and the seals. They will come out in the morning to look around, like old-time sailors, to se[e] what sort of a day it is going to be, and inquire of one another whether it looks like a 'north-easter.[48]

It was a conversation Stephen Norris was eager to join.

---

[48] Captain Rev. Thomas Nangle, *The Trail of The Caribou.*

N.F.L.D. DEPÔT,
NEWTON-ON-AYR,
SCOTLAND.
May 3rd 16

Dear Jack,

I think I sent you some P.C. of the Staff College also a Photo of the bunch. I came back from there on 19th Apl. since then everything is going the same.

A few days ago we, were told to hold ourselves in readiness to move, any moment but we do not know what it, was for, unless it was the Irish Rebellion which, is now settled.

I will wire you before I leave for the front.

How is Fothibull. Hope he is o'k

I find "it", hard to get time to write or I would write more often.

We are dishp busy all day, it is not hard work but, we got to keep moving.

Regards to all

Love to Moll and Kids & Self

from Bud Steel

N.F.L.D. Depot
Newton-On-Ayr
Scotland
May 3rd 16 [underlined]

Dear Jack,

think I sent you some P. C. of the Staff College also a Photo of the bunch. I came back from there on 17th April. Since then everything is going the same. A few days ago we were told to hold ourselves in readiness to move any moment but we do not know which it was for unless it was the Irish Rebellion[49] which is now settled.

I wired Bill a few days ago to ask you to send a donation. I have received it, thanks very much.

I wish they would hurry up and send me out as I am getting fed up with the same thing day in and day out.

What is [Am]Brose Going to do with the Big one. I hope it will work all right.

I suppose every thing is going the same as usual. Anyone enlisting from the French shore? I expect by the time this is over Jim Johnston's group will be called up. Leo Fitzp is still here, he will likely be going with the next lot when ever that will be.

Did you swear the Loyalty Oath, I suppose by the time you get this the Fish will be in, it is summer over here this month.

How are the boys in Goose Cove, I suppose Jack & Matt will be over with the next draft.

Ha Ha.

I will wire you before I leave for the front.

How is [?] hope he is OK.

I find it hard to get time to write or I would write more often.

We are kept busy all day, it is not hard work but we got to keep moving.

Regards to all. Love to Moll and kids & self.

From Brother [?]

Steve

---

[49] Also known as "The Easter Rising," it lasted from April 24 to April 30, 1916.

CHAPTER SIX

A Fellow Can Get Used to Anything

❀

IN the trenches of France, flies had been supplanted by another pest: rats. There were millions of them, brown and black, and they could grow as big as cats. They carried diseases and ate everything, most horribly dead soldiers. Lice persisted here as well, and many soldiers chose to shave their heads to avoid at least the nits, even as they struggled to delouse their uniforms.

Days in the trenches started an hour before dawn, when they assembled for "stand to," positioned in readiness on the fire steps. Although both sides did this routinely and knew each other was doing so in preparation for enemy activity, many attacks still did happen at this time. And then there was the "morning hate," both sides firing off their machine guns in an untargeted flare of anger. This was followed by a shot of rum, inspection, and breakfast. All along the front lines, there were pockets where an unofficial truce was held during this brief time span so soldiers could eat. When the higher-ups learned of such an arrangement, they quickly ordered it discontinued, but these micro-truces happened over and over again all the same.

After breakfast there were inspections and chores. During the day, the soldiers kept as still as possible as any movement could attract swift enemy retaliation. Many newly-arrived soldiers, unable to resist the temptation to peer above the trenches at No Man's Land, were shot on their first day.

Dusk brought another "stand to" and then a chance to move more freely, conduct supply and maintenance operations and patrols, as well as more personal business like writing letters. Sentries guarded in two-hour cycles. A longer stretch would tax their exhaustion, and a man found asleep on sentry duty could be shot. Meanwhile, no one could ever really sleep for any length of time.

But, as the Newfoundland Regiment learned, and Frank "Mayo" Lind— Newfoundland's unofficial war correspondent—wrote in one of his letters to *The Daily News*, "a fellow can get used to anything."[50] In this alien and deeply uncomfortable world, they adapted.

"No pen could describe what it is like, how calmly one stands and faces death, jokes and laughs; everything is just an everyday occurrence," Lind wrote.

> You are mud covered, dry and caked, perhaps, but you look at the chap next [to] you and laugh at the state he is in; then you look down at your own clothes and then the other fellow laughs. Then a whizz bang[51] comes across and misses both of you, and both laugh together.[52]

The 12th Battalion Sherwood Foresters, stationed at Ypres, found an abandoned printing press and published a magazine: *The Wiper Times* (the name echoes the constant mispronunciation of "Ypres"; the Foresters took the press

---

[50] Lind, *The Letters of Mayo Lind*, 141. Mayo Lind was killed July 1, 1916.
[51] Ibid. A gun that shoots shells at high speed: the shells "whizz" as they move through the air.
[52] Ibid.

with them as they moved around the front and changed the publication's title to reflect their current location). The often lampooning material included the following:

Proof That We Are Winning The War, by Belary Helloc[53]

In this article I wish to show plainly that under existing conditions, everything points to a speedy disintegration of the enemy. We will take first of all the effect of war on the male population of Germany. Firstly, let us take as our figures, 12,000,000 as the total fighting population of Germany. Of these 8,000,000 are killed or being killed, hence we have 4,000,000 remaining. Of these 1,000,000 are non-combatants, being in the navy.

Of the 3,000,000 remaining, we can write off 2,500,000 as temperamentally unsuitable for fighting, owing to obesity and other ailments engendered by a gross mode of living. This leaves us 500,000 as the full strength. Of these 497,250 are known to be suffering from incurable diseases. This leaves us 2,750. Of these 2,150 are on the eastern front, and of the remaining 600, 584 are generals and staff.

Thus we find that there are 16 men on the western front. This number, I maintain, is not enough to give them even a fair chance of resisting four more big pushes, and hence the collapse of the western campaign.[54]

The soldiers took part in scouting parties and reconnaissance missions. They were sent out on night patrols in an attempt to capture German soldiers, although by far most of the enemy prisoners of war surrendered after a battle; over

[53] This is a satirical reference to Hilaire Belloc, editor of the pro-war magazine *Land and Water*, which was notable for its inflated estimates of enemy casualties and unbounded optimism.

[54] "The Comedy of War," last modified November 10, 2008, http://www.guardian.co.uk/world/2008/nov/10/first-world-war-humour-wipers-times

700,000 would eventually be interned in Britain and France. Then, moving to Louvencourt, they marched up to the front on June 30. Stephen Norris was now in the ranks.

❀

ON July 1, 1916, the Battle of the Somme began. British and French forces designed the offensive to bring the war to a swift and sure end.

The weather on June 30 had been lovely. At 9 p.m., the Regiment fell in and after roll call marched five hours to Beaumont Hamel. "It is great to see how happy and light-hearted everyone is," Lieutenant Owen Steele wrote, "and yet this is undoubtedly the last day for a good many. The various Battalions marched off whistling and singing, and it was a great sight. Of course this is certainly the best way to take things and hope for the best."

At 2 a.m. they were at St. John's Road, the trench named in the Regiment's honour by 2nd South Wales Borderers. The officers didn't sleep. The men dozed. They had permission to smoke. It was a heightened and eerily familiar atmosphere, "very much like the final few minutes before a big football match," wrote Capt. Arthur Raley.

The plan was to have the Regiment start from St. John's Road, a new trench built by the Regiment, south of Beaumont Hamel. They were to cross two support trenches and our firing line, from which they would pass through the gaps in our wire and across to No Man's Land. They were then to cross the first and second German systems, which were supposed to have been taken by the 86th and 87th Brigades, and halt near Pursiuex Road while artillery weakened the third enemy system, which was the objective that our Regiment was to take possession of.[55]

55 Cramm, *The First Five Hundred*, 57.

July 1, 1916, also dawned a beautiful day.

They readied their arms and steadied their nerves.

At 7:30 a.m. they went over the top. The Germans were waiting for them. The bullets flew like hail, and some men held their hands in front of their faces as if walking through a storm.[56]

It was all over in thirty minutes. "The fire lasted maybe half an hour," soldier Howard Morry recalled. "I don't know, at times like that time doesn't count, you just can't realize how things are."[57]

Only 68 of the Regiment were left to answer the next roll call.

They had suffered a dreadful shock, which left their spirits very low. As soldier Victor Carew wrote from "somewhere in France July 1916... [I]t is quite lonesome here now all my chums are gone I suppose it will be my turn next...."[58] Many felt if their time came up, that was it, and they would be proud to fall for King and country. Over and over the soldiers urged their families not to worry about them.

Stephen Norris was then a Corporal with "F" Company. All the Regiment officers were either killed or wounded at Beaumont Hamel, but he was spared that. He was "On strength"—with the ten percent reserve—as were Captain Donnelley, Lieutenant Steele, and Major Hadow—the 100 or so that were kept back from the fighting and from the front.[59]

The Regiment spent the rest of July trying to regroup. Reinforcements came up on the 11th. That brought troop numbers up to about battalion strength, allowing them to

[56] This image has been cited many times, but its origins are unclear. According to Bert Riggs: "I too have heard or read this description many times but do not know the source."

[57] Howard Morry, quoted in Facey-Crowther, "The Soldier's Tale," 6.

[58] Victor Carew, quoted in Facey-Crowther, "The Soldier's Tale," 7.

take over some front line trenches on the 14th, but they were only there for three or four days. Their position shifted a bit here and there until the next big repositioning in October when they were sent to Gueudecourt.

At that point, they had been away from the fighting for roughly 10 weeks.

❀

HELLFIRE Corner in Belgium was the most dangerous spot on the Flemish Front. It was a vital crossroads for troops and supplies, where the Ypres-Menin road crossed the Ypres-Roulers railway. All visible movement invited shots from German gunners. The British tried to screen themselves with canvas or with darkness. But it remained notoriously hazardous. The only thing to do was pass through the danger zone as quickly as possible. If you were on foot, you ran. If you were on horse, you galloped. If you were in a truck, you pressed the accelerator to the floor.

In August, the Newfoundland Regiment was there. They set up their accommodations alongside the moat, found some shelter in the cellars of L'Ecole, and dug fire trenches. There were only 30 yards between the Newfoundlanders and the German trenches. Within this narrow and underworld geography, Dominion Prime Minister Sir Edward Patrick Morris paid them a visit.

On August 8, a phosgene gas attack was launched. It was the first time the Newfoundlanders faced cloud gas. There were no casualties within the Regiment, but all the transport horses of the Royal Inniskilling Fusiliers died.

[59] 2nd Lt. Sam Ebsary, accordion player, is also in this nominal roll. (Throughout WWI there were four reasons some of the Regiment were held back from the front: as reinforcement after the initial attack; as stretcher bearers, cooks, or other required personnel; as members of the wounded or ill; or as latecomers to the front lines.)

CHAPTER SEVEN

War is Hard to Explain to Someone Who Wasn't There

❀

"How How the time is passing...like a dream...," soldier Lester Barbour wrote from the field. "[Mother] I will try and do my duty as a soldier should, and if I fall, it will be for king and country, as many another brave man has fallen before."[60]

"I did not have my clothes off for 30 days you will... understand how exceptionally busy we were & at last I have had a good dose of the real thing as far as fighting goes," soldier H. G. R. Mews wrote his mother later. "I was very lucky...I alone was the only platoon commander who came out with the Capt."

All the same, Mews was intent on putting his discomfort, and any sense of personal danger, aside to sign off with reassurance:

> It is a lovely evening and I am feeling a most glorious restfulness as I have just come out into the old farm house which is our billet after a most glorious walk in a marvellously quaint and pretty country road...the sunset was as good as any I ever saw in Manuels.[61]

60 Facey-Crowther, "The Soldier's Tale," 6-7.
61 Facey-Crowther, "The Soldier's Tale," 6.

The tremendous noise continued, an annoyance they were acclimatized to. Just as they were accustomed to a month in the same clothes. They scrounged and schemed for a bit of "refreshment" (whisky). They rarely spoke openly of the possibility they could be shot or shelled and killed. Instead, they hoped they wouldn't "be called to go West."

There were exercises and games. In the Brigade Assault at Arms, August 26th, when the drills included revetting trenches, the Newfoundlanders won the Tug of War, against their opponents in the Brigade, in a best of three. There were social events such as a dinner at Hornwork—the famous ruins dating to Louis XV—now decorated with red and white crepe paper. The menu included Potage a la Quidi Vidi, and someone played "The Star of Logy Bay."[62] Then, a Lieutenant, Sam Ebsary, borrowed an accordion and played "The Banks of Newfoundland." The lyrics had been written by Chief Justice Francis Forbes, in 1820, and the piano arrangement published by Oliver Ditson of Boston. It was possibly the first Newfoundland composition set to musical notation. In St. John's, it was much associated with the August Regatta (as was Ebsary, well known as a crewman and cox on the pond). In France, the soldiers of the Newfoundland Regiment made it their own:

> You bully boys of Liverpool
> And I'll have you to beware,
> When you sail on them packet ships,
> no dungaree jackets wear;
> But have a big monkey jacket
> all ready to your hand,
> For there blows some cold nor'westers
> on the Banks of Newfoundland.

---

[62] Nicholson, *The Fighting Newfoundlander*, 300.

We'll scrape her and we'll scrub her
with holy stone and sand,
For there blows some cold nor'westers
on the Banks of Newfoundland.
We had Jack Lynch from Ballynahinch,
Mike Murphy and some more,
And I tell you by's, they suffered like hell
on the way to Baltimore;
They pawned their gear in Liverpool
and they sailed as they did stand,
But there blows some cold nor'westers
on the Banks of Newfoundland.
We'll scrape her and we'll scrub her
with holy stone and sand,
For there blows some cold nor'westers
on the Banks of Newfoundland.
Now the mate he stood on the fo'c'sle head
and loudly he did roar,
Now rattle her in me lucky lads,
you're bound for America's shore;
Come wipe the blood off that dead man's face
and haul or you'll be damned,
But there blows some cold nor'westers
on the Banks of Newfoundland.
We'll scrape her and we'll scrub her
with holy stone and sand,
For there blows some cold nor'westers
on the Banks of Newfoundland.
So now it's reef and reif, me boys
With the Canvas frozen hard
and this mountain pass every Mother's son
on a ninety foot topsail yard

nevermind about boots and oilskins
but holler or you'll be damned
But there blows some cold nor'westers
on the Banks of Newfoundland.
We'll scrape her and we'll scrub her
with holy stone and sand,
And we'll think of them cold nor'westers
on the Banks of Newfoundland.
So now we're off the hook, me boys,
and the land is white with snow,
And soon we'll see the pay table
and we'll spend the whole night below;
And on the docks, come down in flocks,
those pretty girls will say,
Ah, It's snugger with me than on the sea,
on the Banks of Newfoundland.
We'll scrape her and we'll scrub her
with holy stone and sand,
And we'll think of them cold nor'westers
on the Banks of Newfoundland.

They moved on October 6. There was to be another "Push."
The weather turned.

CHAPTER EIGHT

Step Into the Fire, Step Into the Dark

❁

IT was early October 1916, and the Newfoundlanders were back on the Somme. As part of the 88th Brigade, and now attached to the 12th Division, they were in the front line at Gueudecourt. Field Marshal Sir Douglas Haig, Commander of the British Expeditionary Force, was eager to shore up advances in the area and was manoeuvering with the French army to the south. This was part of The Big Push. Fighting started October 7.

The weather that month was terrible, very wet, and the pretty fields were churned to muck. Strafe from the Germans came every night, a dread routine. Everything was cold mud and loud noise, a racket they first thought they would never get used to and then thought they would never really stop hearing, even if The Great War, as it was called from the first, ever ended, even if they ever slept.

On October 8, Stephen Norris was with the Newfoundland Regiment as they boarded a train near Ypres.

Disembarking, they marched from Longeau to Corbie. The road was very busy with soldiers, horses, ambulances. The German planes flew overhead. Each soldier carried 70 lbs of gear: kit bags, grenades, picks, shovels, wire cutters, gas helmets, ammunitions, and rifles.

After midnight on October 9, the 88th Brigade filed into 21 charabancs for a long, cold ride from Combie. It was 16 miles to the battle area. On the way to Gueudecourt, they received directions from a polite man in British uniform, a passing British captain, who pointed the correct direction, and whom one Newfoundlander later identified as Edward, Prince of Wales.[63]

Around dawn, they crossed the line broken by the British on July 1. There was not a building left, not a tree. All the living and fabricated ecology was military: there were soldiers, horses, equipment, and supplies. Their slow momentum winnowed to 5 mph. They were three miles from the firing line.

❀

In the Field
10.10.16

Dear Jack,

Here we are still fit and well T. G. [thank God] but busy, busier than we have been at all, we are pushing the Germans back so, we will be doing a bit of moving and incidentally a bit of fighting. How much depends, of course, Ha Ha.

I am writing this now in a place that the British were a few weeks ago and where we are still advancing, we will be in the thick of it very soon, and we expect to do well.

Kind regards to all relatives and friends

Love to Moll, Self and Kids

From [?].
Steve

---

[63] Nicholson, *The Fighting Newfoundlander*, 306.

In the Field
10.10.16

Dear Jack,

Here we are still fit & well T.G but busy, busier than we have been at all. We are pushing the Germans back so we will be doing a bit of moving and incidently a bit of fighting. How much depends of course. Ha. Ha.

I am writing this now in a place that the British won a few weeks ago and where we are still advancing, we will in the thick of it very soon, and we expect to do well.

Kind regards to all Relations & Friends.

Love to Moll self & Kids.

From yours —

Theo

❀

GUEUDECOURT, October 12, was to be Allied Commander General Sir Douglas Haig's renewal of the Somme Offensive. The July Drive was acknowledged a complete failure, one so final it marked a turning point in Allied strategy. Never again would waves of soldiers be sent out of trenches towards enemy gunfire.

British military leaders tried to find new ways to strike. They experimented with night attacks. Then, on September 15, 1916, came the first use of tanks at the battle of Flers-Courcelette. The "Land Battleships" looked formidable but had a rocky debut. 49 were ordered but only 32 delivered, and seven of those could not be started in time. The engineers behind the project had warned the tanks weren't ready, and there was great trepidation in unleashing such a forceful secret weapon in a slightly tepid way. But Haig insisted on using them.

Overall, the Allies had partial success but then bogged down. As did most Battle of the Somme attacks in that period, after advancing just so far beyond enemy lines, both enemy and allied soldiers were stuck with their supply systems broken down and all progress stagnated as the opposing forces brought in reinforcements and counterattacked. Nobody could get more than one or two kilometres.

The Allies also started experimenting with a new way of using their artillery, their big guns. It was called a creeping barrage—"barrage" from the French "to fire". This would be used at Gueudecourt. The idea was to create a scrim of artillery fire that moved ahead 50 yards every 30 seconds (this was later adjusted to 100 yards every three minutes) with the infantry coming close behind it. The idea was that the exploding shells forced the enemy to keep their heads down, neutralizing them. The Allies found the tactic would increase the number of friendly fire casualties, but decrease the total number of Allied casualties.

For the most part, it was not successful. Only one of all the British units involved at Gueudecourt captured all its goals— the 1st Battalion. The Newfoundlanders. They seized not only their own objectives but part of another unit's as well.

There was a lot of motivation. This was revenge for Beaumont Hamel.

❀

ON the first four days of October, the Regiment set the clocks back an hour, noted a downed enemy observation balloon, had a private punished for sleeping on duty, and were relieved by the 5th Kings Liverpool.

On the 10th, they moved into trenches north of the town of Gueudecourt. Stephen Norris wrote a letter home.

On October 11, they bivouacked on grounds replete with German ammunition. The very earth was raked by war. Someone set off a bomb that injured four.

The night was fine and cold. They were dug in on the northern outskirts, and company commanders met with Colonel Hadow at his headquarters to the south of town. They were given battle orders.

But the battle had already begun.

That night, Lieutenant Stephen C. Norris, of "C" Company (88th Brigade), regiment number 921, was killed by a shell. Eight other men died with him when their trench blew in.

❀

AT 2 p.m. October 12, the order came. The Regiment went over the top and advanced under a line of artillery—that new Allied strategy of a creeping barrage.[64] The shells did provide a screen. But 10% of the advancing soldiers were killed by their own artillery.

"The day was marked by heroic and daring conduct, and by the loss of some of the very finest of the Regiment," read one report.[65] "It was a glorious but sad day for the Regiment, for here were lost Captains O'Brien and Donnelly, and Lieutenants Cecil Clift, Steve Norris and Sam Ebsary—all gallant officers," said another.[66]

"[Mother] Here I am, managed to do the trick at last, such a lovely blighty wound," wrote Rupert Bartlett.

> It is only a matter of waiting for the wound to heal, and I will be O.K. again. We certainly had a lovely time! The advance was a great success. We got into the German bunch almost before he knew we were coming. Tell Wilf a day's partridge shooting was small sport compared with it. I don't know how many we shot running away. I got hit early in the afternoon just as I reached the French but did not come in until about 8 that night. I got bruised up badly in fact could hardly walk. So that's why I partly came down.[67]

Altogether, 120 of the Regiment died there, and 119 were wounded. It was the third worst battle for the Regiment: the

[64] "With the aid of lantern slides, the audience was given a splendid idea of the creeping barrage, which "combs the hair" of the advancing troops, and shown how it acts. The French, who first adopted it, are now using a new barrage, which is thrown beyond the enemy's trench, and slowly creeps towards their own lines. The effect of this is to drive the Bosches into surrendering; but they must be sure to leave their arms behind them if they hope to get in safely." Captain Rev. Thomas Nangle, *The Trail of the Caribou*, report of Nangle's lecture given October 19th, 1917.

[65] Cramm, *The First Five Hundred*, 63.

[66] Captain Rev. Thomas Nangle, The Trail of the Caribou. Report of Nangle's lecture given October 19th, 1917.

[67] Facey-Crowther, "The Soldier's Tale," 6.

toll at Beaumont Hamel was higher, and the toll at Cambrai was higher. Stephen Norris was one of 38 bodies never found.

❁

THE Somme Offensive lasted four months and cost 600,000 Allied casualties. With the German casualties included, the number was over a million. It was the worst battle in the War and, in fact, one of the most costly in military history. And it was futile. No significant advancements were made. Victory remained elusive. Many would blame Haig.

On October 24, 1916, Stephen Norris was promoted "to be Lieutenant. The above promotion to date from July 12, 1916. ([S]ince Killed in Action October 12, 1916.)"

Of 4212 Newfoundlanders on the Western Front, 1300 died. Total fatalities in the War amounted to 1.22% of Newfoundland's male population.

❁

16th October, 1916.

Dear Sir,

I regret to inform you that the Record Office of the First Newfoundland Regiment, London, to-day advises that 2nd Lieut. S. C. Norris was Killed in Action on the 12th October.

Yours faithfully,

Colonial Secretary
[To] Mr. James Norris,
c/o Mr. W. H. Jackman,[68]
City.

❁

[68] James Norris's son-in-law, married to his daughter, Nell.

18th October, 1916

Dear Sir,

It was with the greatest possible regret that I learned from the official casualty lists that your son, Second Lieutenant Stephen C. Norris, was Killed in Action on October 12th, and I wish to express to you and your family my sincerest sympathy in your time of sorrow.

In your bereavement I feel sure that you will find consolation in the thought that you[r] son willingly answered the call of King and Country, and gave his life in defence of the principles of Righteousness, Truth and Liberty, and that his name will be inscribed upon the glorious Hall of Honour and will be held in fragrant memory by all his fellow-countrymen.

With sincerest sympathy,

I am,

Yours faithfully,

[To] Mr. James Norris
c/o Mr. W. H. Jackman
Colonial Secretary
LeMarchant Road

❀

27th October, 1916.

Dear Sir,

I beg to inform you that a report has just been received from the Record Office of the First Newfoundland Regiment, London, to the effect that it has been ascertained that

the date on which you[r] son, Lieutenant S. C. Norris, was killed was October 11th, and not October 12th, as was first reported.

Yours faithfully,

Colonial Secretary
[To] Mr. James Norris,
Three Arms,
N. D. B.

❀

28 October 1916
To Jas Norris
Care Jackman
Water Street West
St. John's (Newfoundland)

(Telegram) Western Union
Anglo-American Direct United States
Cablegram
Via Western Union
To Jas Norris
Care Jackman

Water Street West St Johns (Newfoundland)

*STEVE KILLED ELEVEN A M OCTOBER ELEVENTH
BY BIG SHELL WHOLE TRENCH FELL IN BODY NOT
FOUND AM ON THE GROUND MYSELF DOING
EVERYTHING POSSIBLE TO LOCATE BODY ALL WERE
AT CONFESSION DAY BEFORE DONNELLY SHOT ON
GERMAN PARAPET OBRIEN WOUNDED STOMACH
LIVED FOR WEEK AM LONGSIDE OUR BOYS HEARTFELT
SYMPATHY TO SELF MOTHER NELL AND FAMILY.*

Rev Tom Nangle
Via synoptical [handwritten]
File/Send Collect

[handwritten copy also on file]

❀

IN Stephen Norris's Regiment papers, under Field Service, and stamped Nov 13, 1916, is the following text:

Died: Place or Hospital, *In the Field, France.*

Cause of Death, *Killed in Action.*

Place of Burial, *Not to Hand.*

CHAPTER NINE

His Very Fine Example

❀

FROM the *Newfoundland Regiment War Diary*:[69]

10/10/16 At night the regiment moved into first line trenches in front of Gueudecourt. The battalion was heavily shelled while in the trenches before the attack and suffered casualties including 2/Lieut S. C. Norris (killed).

12/10/16 The attack took place at 14.05...Capt. Donnelley was killed on reaching the trench.[70]

During the battle three machine guns were captured also taken prisoners 2 Officer, 1 W. O. and some 56 men.

Our total casualties for the whole time from going into the trenches were Officers 19, O. R. 229. Estimated casualties of enemy 250 killed.

Stephen Norris was a St. Bonaventure alumnus and the school's paper, *Adelphian*, noted his loss. He was one of 16

---

[69] Excerpt from *The Newfoundland Regiment War Diary*. Private collection of John Wheeler.

[70] Donnelly, Stephen Norris's friend from St. Bonaventure's, was the first member of the Regiment to be awarded the Military Cross. He died less than a day after Stephen Norris fell. 2nd Lieut. Sam Ebsary died of his wounds on October 15.

graduates slain to that date (and eight were reported missing in action).

He had entered the college in 1908, graduating in 1911 with thoughts of a career in medicine, the paper noted:

> [B]ut his father's extensive business had the most attraction for him, and he was thus employed and giving promise of becoming a very successful business man when the call for men went forth. Donning the Khaki, he soon made his mark as a leader and became a very efficient and popular officer. He stood high in the estimation of the soldiers under him, and just prior to sailing for England, his platoon presented him with an address and a suitable present in recognition of his services as trainer and of the esteem in which he was held.

> While at the Front in France his leadership was again conspicuous and those estimable qualities for which he was noted soon attracted the attention of his superior officers, one of whom, Lieut.-Col Hadow, writing to the father, says in part: "He was killed instantaneously by a big shell just as he was trying to rescue a man who had been buried by another shell. His platoon had had a particularly bad time through very heavy shelling and there were only three survivors, and your son stuck to his trench in the most gallant manner. He was a most promising officer and I deeply regret his loss. The only consolation I can offer you is that by his very fine example he helped to hold our trench under very heavy shell fire and this enabled us [...] contributed in no small measure to the success of the Regiment."

The foregoing extract epitomizes Steve's noble qualities as a gallant officer, and although we find no V.C. or D.C.M. after his name to tell of his gallantry, we know that he valiantly played the game and that the memory of his valor will endure as long as there is one of his platoon left to tell of the heroic action in which he took such a prominent and honoured part.

He was in his 25th year and like his college friend, Capt. J. Donnelly, he now sleeps the sleep of the brave "somewhere in France." To all old pupils, especially those of his class-period, we would ask a remembrance in their prayers for the eternal rest of our fallen hero.[71]

As the *Adelphian* recounted, Stephen Norris had expressed an intention to go to medical school. It is quite probable he could have done this as Thomas Roddick of Harbour Grace was Dean of Medicine at McGill, and any Newfoundlanders who applied and showed some merit were admitted. But, following his graduation from St. Bonaventure's, he went back to Three Arms and worked at the family business. Perhaps he planned to do that for a couple of years and then focus on a medical career. If so, he would never get that chance.

❁

IN January 1918, the Regiment was awarded the designation "Royal," the only such designation made during WWI.

[71] *Adelphian* 14:1 (1917).

CHAPTER TEN

Raise the Soldiers, Bury the Dead

❁

THE Regiment's losses in the summer and fall of 1916 did not mean that Newfoundland men stopped volunteering to fight—nor did it stem the propaganda urging them to do so:

An Appeal

From His Excellency the Governor for Recruits for Active Service

"I am addressing this appeal to all the people of New-foun[d]land, but especially to those of the Outports.

Your Government have decided to make another special attempt to obtain further recruits for the duties forced upon us by the war. I am anxious to explain to you in simple and strong words why those duties are yours.

In your sea-girt home you have, I know, your own dangers and anxieties to face. As I write this my mind is still full of the appalling disaster to the "Florizel." But war you do not realize; you are beyond the sound of the guns...That awe inspiring rumble of the guns which I ask you to imagine – that lurid light on the horizon which I ask you to picture – are the signs of a terrible struggle for Right- of a mighty effort to save from ruin, not only France, but every bit of free soil in the world, including this Island of which you are so proud...By some permission of Divine Providence, which we do not understand, a nation of criminals is now attacking all that is just and true in the whole world. Germany has set herself deliberately to violate every law of Right and every principle of Humanity. Never before in history had war been planned like this...As Judas treated Christ, Germany is treating civilization...The German nation today knows no law except that of the pagan, the liar, the ravisher, the murderer. They are a curse...And the task demanded of us is to fight and conquer Sin...Remember that your wives, your children, your cottage, your boats are in positive danger if the Germans break through in France. As he is treating the foolish Russians, so he will treat every nation whom he touches – America, Canada, New-foundland...He is entirely evil...This mass of incarnate selfishness is held back by the strong arm of the Allies in France. Will any man of British race decline to do all he can to defeat and crush it?..."

C. Alexander Harris,
Governor and Commander-in-Chief
Government House, St. John's, March 30th, 1918[72]

The same publication carried information from the Minister of Militia, J. R. Bennett, on sending parcels to "Prisoners of War in Germany!" Food was permitted three times a fort-night, clothing—great coat, trousers, cap, drawers (woollen), undervest (woollen), towels, handkerchiefs, boots—period-ically, and money was inadvisable "unless P. of W. ask for it. The amount which may be sent is Two Shillings per week per any one man."[73]

[72] Quoted in Nangle, *The Trail of the Caribou.*
[73] Ibid.

September 6th, 1918.

James Norris, Esq.,
Three Arms, N. D. B.

Dear Sir,-
I enclose herewith cheque for $43.35,
being the balance of the Estate of your late son,
Lieutenant Stephen Norris, due to you as Administrator.
I also enclose letter of Administration.

Yours faithfully,
Capt & Paymaster

❊

NOVEMBER 1918, at the eleventh hour of the eleventh day of the eleventh month, the Armistice was signed. The Regiment, now the Royal Newfoundland Regiment, were at Harlebeke, Belgium. On December 4, they entered Germany as part of the Army of Occupation. On February 14, 1919, they withdrew to England, joined the 2nd Battalion, and marched in the Victory Parade in London on May 3. On July 1, 1919, they were back in Newfoundland.

No one is really sure of the total number of soldiers who died in WWI, of the total of casualties from England and France and Germany, and Austria-Hungary, and Australia and New Zealand, and Africa and the Caribbean, and Portugal and Turkey and the United States. Ten million? Add civilian deaths and the count of dead and injured is likely more than 35 million.

For Newfoundland it was about 1300 men. The Regiment's volunteers had a fatality rate of 26% and a casualty rate of 70%.

WWI left Newfoundland with a debt of $13 million.

❀

Sep 9 1921 [stamp]

The accompanying Victory Medal and/or British War
Medal is/are forwarded herewith to
Mr. James Norris (Father)
in respect of his services as No – Rank Lieut.
Name Stephen C. Norris Royal Nfld. Regt.
Receipt of the same should be acknowledged hereon.
[handwritten]
Received Victory & B War Medal
Signature James Norris
Date Oct 11th 1921
Address Three Arms N D Bay

Receipt of a Memorial Plaque is acknowledged the same day.

❀

ANTHEM FOR DOOMED YOUTH

What passing-bells for these who die as cattle?
Only the monstrous anger of the guns.
Only the stuttering rifles' rapid rattle
Can patter out their hasty orisons.
No mockeries for them; no prayers nor bells,
Nor any voice of mourning save the choirs, –
The shrill, demented choirs of wailing shells;
And bugles calling for them from sad shires.
What candles may be held to speed them all?
Not in the hands of boys, but in their eyes
Shall shine the holy glimmers of goodbyes.
The pallor of girls' brows shall be their pall;
Their flowers the tenderness of patient minds,
And each slow dusk a drawing-down of blinds.

    – by Wilfred Owen[74]

❀

THE Royal Newfoundland Regiment officially disbanded on August 26, 1919.[75] It had had one purpose, now served.

Major Arthur Raley:

I recall handing in the colours at Government House, Newfoundland, marching to a parade ground I'd never been on, near the old skating rink. I fancy a hotel is built there now. The whole regiment formed up...[The commanding officer] said: 'The regiment dismissed' and they all swarmed, the men with their rifles, swarmed to their sons, daughters, aunts, mothers and so on and I said [to the CO], 'You've got a house to go to, haven't you?' He said, 'Yes'. I didn't know where to go. I went into lodgings. Nothing happened. I was just an ordinary individual. That was the end of the war as far as I was concerned.[76]

❀

July 21st 19
Principal Secretary
Imperial War Graves Commission
Winchester House
St. James Square
London S.W.1.

Sir:
It has been found that there are a number of bodies and

---

[74] Wilfred Owen, *Wilfred Owen: The War Poems*, ed. Jon Stallworthy, (London: Chatto & Windus, 1994), 12.

[75] As did the Newfoundland Forestry Corps.

[76] David R. Facey-Crowther ed. *Lieutenant Owen William Steele of the Newfoundland Regiment, Diary and Letters*, (Montreal and Kingston: McGill-Queen's University Press, 2002), 10.

graves of Newfoundland soldiers which have not been registered and of which the location is not officially known. The Government desire that all these as well as isolated registered graves of Newfoundland soldiers should be collected into the Military Cemeteries which are now being formed in Belgium and France.

Major Thos. Nangle,[77] C. F., who has been attached to the Royal Newfoundland Regiment for the last three years has personal knowledge of most of these graves and has been detailed to undertake the work of temporary marking the unregistered graves and seeing that they are ultimately placed in those cemeteries, and it is possible that you may be able to place a motor car and other facilities at his disposal. He has been authorized to incur the necessary expenditure in order to have this work satisfactorily carried out.

It would be deemed a courtesy if your commission would assist him in carrying out this important work,

I have the honour to be,

Sir,

Your obedient servant,

Minister of Militia

C.R. 0-20

❀

JAMES and Mary Norris, along with their daughter, Nell, went to France after the war ended to look for Stephen Norris's body. But it was never found. The name of Stephen Norris is inscribed at Beaumont Hamel.

---

[77]   Officially, Sir Edgar Bowring was the representative on the War Graves Commission, but Nangle was an animated force of his own.

JAMES, ELLEN, AND MARY NORRIS in 1917. The three members of the Norris family travelled to the battlefield in France in search of Stephen's remains, but his body was never recovered.

EPILOGUE

❁

THE Commission of Government (1933-1949) was not popular on Three Arms Island, and the older generation was opposed to Confederation. They were an independent-minded community, but not free from the influence of larger, outside forces.

In 1911, there were 54 people; in 1921, 47; in 1935, 25; in 1945, 12; in the 1950s, 4 or 5; and in December 1956 the last of the Moores and Wellses and Batstones left. Many other young men had enlisted in WWI, and then WWII, and over the decades many of the young women had left for Corner Brook or farther afield to pursue their work or education.

Without Stephen Norris, there was no one in the family to take over the Three Arms branch of the business, and no other merchant moved to the island. James Norris died in 1924, and John (Jack) Norris died only ten days later. The family was diminishing. None of the children stayed in Three Arms, and Nell and her mother left Newfoundland. Under resettlement, the remaining families floated their homes to other towns, like Harry's Harbour, and the memory of Three Arms ebbed in their wake.

The myth that the death of Stephen Norris was directly responsible for the effacement of Three Arms was just that, a myth, but one with a core of truth. Certainly Stephen Norris was supposed to take over the Three Arms business, as his brother John had in Conche, and Bernard in Coachman's Cove, while Ambrose took charge of the schooners. The scythe of war intervened, and Stephen Norris's death became the sign that presaged the loss of Three Arms. It is possible the facts of Stephen Norris's life became somewhat entangled in the fate of Three Arms Island's population because there was correspondence. Stephen Norris volunteered for the Regiment, and he was killed. Within decades, Three Arms did pass away; you can see the census drop, year by year, until a post-Confederation count yields but two. This was an arc symbolic of what happened to so much of Newfoundland, *what befell*. Because of the War…if not for the War….

No one foresaw this, this price, this horizon. Not any government, not any soldier. "They were expecting it to be over by Christmas first of all, they signed up for a year, they were frightened to death that it was going to be over by the time they got there," said Riggs. "This was seen very much as an adventure. And I don't think a single one of them thought they were going to be killed. They were going over there to teach the Hun a lesson. And they were going to be back. Until they hit the trenches and saw what it was actually like, there was none of them that believed that this was anything but an adventure. Once they hit the trenches, it became a tragedy."

❁

IN 1962, Royal Newfoundland Regiment Veteran Howard Morry was interviewed on CBC radio. Morry, a fisherman and farmer, had volunteered with the second wave of recruits. On July 1, 1916, he had been seconded to provide rations for the advancing troops, an order he said "vexed" him at the time as it kept him away from the action. He hadn't organized even a first round of provisions when he realized that there was no one left to bring them to.

Forty-eight years later, he said,

> You can look back and think. I often think what wonderful kids they were. You take a lot of them, were sixteen and seventeen and eighteen years old. I was one of the old fellows [30] and I often wondered at the bravery of them little kids. No stopping them at all, go wherever they were sent, do whatever they were told and laugh about it.[78]

[78] Howard Morry, quoted in Facey-Crowther, "The Soldier's Tale," 11.

PART TWO

❀

2004.

Also a leap year.

UNESCO declares the International Year to Commemorate the Struggle Against Slavery. Queen Elizabeth II christens the RM.S *Queen Mary 2*—the largest passenger ship in the world. Vladimir Putin handily wins his second term as Russian President, while George W. Bush wins a closer race to retain the American Oval Office. Facebook, the social networking site developed by Mark Zuckerberg, is incorporated. Armed bandits steal Edvard Munch's *The Scream*, *Madonna*, and other masterpieces from the Munch Museum in Oslo. (*The Scream* was later recovered and, in 2012, fetched a record $119.9 Million US at auction.)

Johnny Ramone, Estee Lauder, Ronald Reagan, and Ray Charles die; Dutch filmmaker Theo van Gogh, whose film *Submission* was the subject of much controversy, is assassinated. Over 230,000 people in fourteen countries are killed by the Boxing Day tsunami.

Newfoundland and Labrador Premier Danny Williams, furious with the federal government's position on shares of offshore royalties, orders all Canadian flags removed from the provincial administration's buildings. Newfoundlander Rick Hillier is named commander of the International Security Assistance Force in Afghanistan.

134 million babies, give or take, are born—4598 in New-foundland and Labrador, about half as many as in 1983.

It is ninety years since the First World War began. On a human scale, this is four generations; much more than a lifetime has passed. And yet there are connections and echoes, not just family bonds and associations but historical and political repercussions—Newfoundland's loss of self-government in 1933 being one very direct example—that bridge even the modern-day province to 1914-1918 and all that ensued.

These effects were personal, collective, and cultural. Stephen Norris died, and that anguished his family. And, because he was gone, because he was not there, the work that he was supposed to do, with the family concerns, with his life, was never done. And that left a gap which widened until all the commerce and all the people of Three Arms Island fell in.

It was a sad story, a tragedy that was not forgotten. It was repeated and recorded and even exaggerated over the next decades. And, in the early 20th century, it began to take on an unexpected life of its own.

❀

A Call To Arms
AN ORIGINAL
MUSICAL PRODUCTION

PROGRAMME
2005

THREE ARMS ISLAND AND THE NORRIS FAMILY:
An Oral History [79]

The following is composed of interviews with, in order:

Gary Follett, parent of Gonzaga Theatre Arts student Emily Follett

Jacinta Mackey-Graham, Gonzaga Theatre Arts teacher

Jaakob Palasvirta, Gonzaga Theatre Arts student, who played James Norris

Sarah Loveys, Gonzaga Theatre Arts student, who played Mary Norris

John Wheeler, son of Agnes Norris, who was Stephen Norris's niece

Elizabeth Burry, parent of Gonzaga Theatre Arts student Nick Burry

Emily Follett, Gonzaga Theatre Arts student, who played Sophie (Stephen Norris's fictional girlfriend)

Alicia Eaton, daughter of Bernard Norris, and Stephen Norris's niece

Gonzaga High School, founded in 1962 in St. John's, is located on Smithville Crescent and has a student enrollment of about 655. The school has a well-earned reputation for its musical and theatre productions. Usually these are classic, often Broadway, shows in the style of Guys and Dolls, *staged at the St. John's Arts and Culture Centre, one of the biggest theatrical venues in the province. But in 2004 they decided to do something a little different.*

Teacher Jacinta Mackey-Graham and the 3200 Theatre Arts class at Gonzaga decided to research, write, and present a musical of their own. It would be about a soldier in the First World War. The title was A Call to Arms.

---

[79] These interviews were conducted separately and have been edited into a single piece.

A Call to Arms *was based on the life and death of Stephen Norris, or at least as much as those involved understood the facts at that time: that Stephen Norris's decision to enlist had ended his life as well as his community's existence and his family's connections to it.*

Gary Follett (parent): What happened in Three Arms happened in many places. The story repeated itself in many places.

The production would have an amazing reach and resonance.

The cast included: Maddy Babij, Amanda Blackwood, Josh Bourden (Stephen Norris), Nick Burry, Margaret Casey, Matt Constantine, Keelia Farrell, Emily Follett (Sophie), Sarah Hann, Ryan Hopkins, Doug Jewer, Lisa Kehoe, Andrew Lahey, Sarah Loveys (Mary Norris), Jennifer Murphy, Jake Palasvirta (James Norris), Joanna Parsons, Elizabeth Pitt, Stephen Porter, Adam Power, Nicole Power, Cassidy Quinton, Anna Smith, Kim Sparkes, Emily Thompson, John Walsh, Jeremy Wells, Samantha Whittle, John Williams.

It was directed by Petrina Bromley *and* Jacinta Mackey-Graham. *The original music was by* Ged Blackmore

In the opening scene, four campers from St. John's arrive on an abandoned island in Notre Dame Bay. Their mission: to complete an overnight camping expedition in fulfillment of their Duke of Edinburgh Award. Their guide is nowhere to be seen.[80]

Jacinta Mackey-Graham (Theatre Arts teacher, Gonzaga High School): After we had done *Music Man* in 2001 and then *Oklahoma!* in 2003, I had mentioned to the vice-principal of the school that I felt we had a particularly talented group,

---

[80]   These descriptions of the play are from the publicity materials of "The Original Gonzaga Cast Recording, *A Call to Arms.*"

and I'd like to put them in a class together. Normally we did shows every two years, so the next one wouldn't be until 2005. I didn't want that opportunity to go by. So I proposed to him that I would stack a class, and take the 20, 25 of the best students and put them there together and do something. His suggestion was, "Well, why don't you do something about Tommy Ricketts?" In his office was a big picture of Tommy Rickets. I thought that was a good idea. He was the [youngest] to win the Victoria Cross, so, sounds like a noble venture. That was the premise.

Jaakob Palasvirta (played James Norris, Stephen Norris's father): Tommy Ricketts. The youngest to ever win the Victoria Cross. We started with Tommy Ricketts. On the outset, that looks to be a good thing for a high school production because he's so young, and we could relate to it.

Jacinta Mackey-Graham: I remember telling [Jaakob Palasvirta and Emily Follett] please sign up; we're going to do something amazing. We just don't know what that's going to be yet.

Sarah Loveys (played Mary Norris, Stephen Norris's mother): It turned out to be the most important show we did, the most meaningful one.

Jacinta Mackey-Graham: Over the summer [of 2003] I met with Mary Philpott, and she had done a lot of research into the role of women in the First World War and come across various stories. And I knew that my class was probably going to be three quarters female, so I needed to have something other than the Tommy Ricketts story to make this work. The idea was that we were going to write some script ourselves, take some research and something [about] Newfoundland [history], and write it ourselves. But it would just be way too daunting to think about writing the music as well. So I approached Ged Blackmore. Ged had written lots of music for

pageant-type things around Newfoundland. So he came to
the house with his cousin, Mary Philpott. I was thinking we
were going to be talking about the Tommy Ricketts story.
But Mary said, "According to the research I've done, you're
going to meet a dead end. Yes, he did get the Victoria Cross,
but when he came back he never talked about it anymore."
She proposed this story she had found in her research, about
the Norris family. And she said, "I think that would make a
better premise."

JAAKOB PALASVIRTA AS JAMES NORRIS AND SARAH LOVEYS
AS MARY NORRIS in the Gonzaga High School Production
of *A Call to Arms*.

John Wheeler (son of Agnes Norris, who was John's daughter and Stephen's niece): I grew up sort of vaguely knowing I had an uncle who died in the war. I was too young to know, too young to appreciate. You sort of gleaned things as you grew up.

Jacinta Mackey-Graham: [Mary Philpott] said Stephen Norris defied his father [and] went to the First World War. They were a merchant class family. The father had planned on the son, Stephen, taking over the business. And when Stephen went to war and was killed, the story is that the father died of a broken heart, the business with no one to run it went into receivership, and the people moved away from the island. So essentially the [story arc was the] death of the son, the death of the father, the death of the island.

That's where we started with it, and then we included in that the role of the VAD [Voluntary Aid Detachment, who served as field nurses]. That's how it got going.

Sarah Loveys: We weren't sure what direction it would take. That was quite a complicated process.

Jacinta Mackey-Graham: It really got convoluted. We were doing the research, and all our stories started running into each other. And everybody got very territorial. So then we decided we've got to make this...what's the most compelling? And we went with the Stephen Norris story.

Sarah Loveys: Then it turned into Stephen Norris.

Jaakob Palasvirta: We gained the angle of having the community to tell the story.

Sarah Loveys: More characters.

Jacinta Mackey-Graham: [But we still] couldn't see our path. I'd directed, but I'd never written anything before. It was despairing. They were all very passionate. There was a lot of ownership.

Jaakob Palasvirta: We were doing research into all the different fronts, all the different kinds of stories we could tell in this show. The nurses, the VADs, the community, what it was like to be a soldier. We were really struggling. We were writing little bits of scenes and trying them out.

Sarah Loveys: The difficult part was piecing it all together.

Jaakob Palasvirta: That was when [actor and director] Petrina Bromley came in.

Jacinta Mackey-Graham: I called Petrina one night. I said, "I'm just overwhelmed. This is the amount of research we've got." I had about a two-hour conversation with her on the phone. She was asking me, "Why would the students be invested in this? Why would city kids care about these bay guys?" I said, "Well, they'll go to an island." And she said, "Well, why would they go?" And I said, "Duke of Edinburgh!" because that was the bane of my existence when I was teaching at Gonzaga. Every time I needed to have a rehearsal: "Oh, no, we got Duke of Edinburgh. We got to do an overnight." So she said, "OK, that's fine, they've got to do an overnight." It's like it started then. I said, "So they're going to go to this island, for the Duke of Edinburgh stuff." And she said, "So somebody's going to meet them." And I said, "OK, right, a guide, a guide is going to meet them…." By the time I got off the phone to her, not only did we have the premise of the story, the outline, we knew there were going to be campers, they were going to go to the island, the guide doesn't show up, and this mysterious man meets them, and they say, "so are you our guide?" And, by the time I got off the phone, Tom, my husband, who was listening to this, he had decided that this was going to be called *A Call to Arms.* He said, "These students are called to Three Arms Island, just as Stephen Norris was called to arms."

John Wheeler: What can I tell you about Steve? He grew up in Three Arms. He came in to St. John's to go to school at St. Bonaventure's. The story goes that he did decide to enlist against his parent's wishes.

Jaakob Palasvirta: We had a direction, and soon after that we had a script.

Jacinta Mackey-Graham: Petrina came in, and in that week she worked with their ideas, improvisation. One of the things she had said to me when I told her, the gist of it, was that Stephen dies, his father dies, and the island dies: "it's a fucking depressing story." So she put comedy in there. The story itself doesn't have that. It came by way of the campers.

Jaakob Palasvirta: And that was the key which wove all the little bits together and had quite a bit of original material.

Sarah Loveys: She really helped us shape our ideas. To simplify. We were a big class of great ideas coming from everyone, and it was really difficult to harness all those ideas, to make a story, and fit them into an hour and a half.

The campers meet Solomon Strong, boat builder and storyteller, who welcomes them to Three Arms Island and promises them an interesting stay.

Elizabeth Burry (parent): So the kids wake up on this camping trip, and this guy is there. And they just think he's some skipper who's showed up, but this is [boat builder] Solomon Strong who's come back to tell them the story because they're camping on Three Arms Island.

Sarah Loveys: And that was the ghost story.

The campers awake to bustling activity on the community wharf. Solomon points out James Norris, a successful merchant who is the lifeblood of the community. We meet Stephen, the merchant's son, who is determined to enlist in the New-

foundland Regiment. His girlfriend, Sophie, worries about his safety.

John Wheeler: [Steve] was not at Gallipoli. He was in Scotland. He did not participate on July 1st. He was in the reserve.

It is now October, 1916. The soldiers are ordered to the front lines at Gueudecourt, France. The regiment is bombarded by enemy shellfire. Stephen is mortally wounded. Back on Three Arms Island, the family's worst fears are confirmed: Stephen has been killed. James Norris, devastated by his son's death, loses all interest in the family business and dies of a broken heart a short time later. Mary stays in the community for many years but, as an old woman, realizes the time has come for her to leave.

John Wheeler: He participated in the battle of Gueudecourt. The battle itself was on October 12th. But he died on October 11th. It was enemy shelling. His body was never recovered. His parents, and Nell, went over to look, to try and find his body, with no success.

The play was produced in May 2004. And that should have been the end of it. But, somehow, the Theatre Arts class and their teacher didn't feel ready to let the story go. They still kept thinking about Stephen Norris and his family and the abandoned island. It haunted them. Just a bit, but distinctly. Then…

Elizabeth Burry: Jacinta got it into her head—

Gary Follett: That it would be a good idea to go to Three Arms.

Jacinta Mackey-Graham: I said to [the students one] day, "I don't know about you, but this summer I'm going out there. I'm going to go to Harry's Harbour [the nearest embarkation point] and I'm getting out to Three Arms Island." And Emily said—

Emily Follett (played Sophie, Stephen Norris's girlfriend): Not without us you don't.

Jacinta Mackey-Graham: That's where it started.

Gary Follett: The kids came home and said, "We want to do this, but we need some adults with us, so who can come?" Of course, it was right up my line. I've grown up in the country. I spend 40-weekends-plus a year in the country. The thought of going to some island in Newfoundland and camping for a night was fabulous.

Elizabeth Burry: Didn't know what you were in for, did you?

Jacinta Mackey-Graham: I thought, "What am I doing? I don't even know how to light a Coleman stove." [But] that was the premise of the trip. We made tentative plans, contacted people in the community, to see if there was someone we could hire a boat [from to take us over], because we knew the island was abandoned, and they put us in touch with someone in Grand Falls, Selby Knight. He had a house in Harry's Harbour, and he also had a fairly big vessel. So then we made the decision to go there.

We left on a Friday. When I had contacted the people out there, I said we need a place to stay. They said we could rent the community centre, [the] parish hall, in Harry's Harbour. But then we got this, "Now what would you be wanting to come out here for?" Definitely skepticism. When I said I was taking a bunch of teenagers, you know they weren't thinking the best. So I told them this story. "*Yes, but why would you want to go to the island?*"

Elizabeth Burry: It wasn't just the play, it was the whole weekend. And for the kids to go and see that island and see nobody living there but know that all this stuff happened.

Jacinta Mackey-Graham: And I explained that. And I said is there any chance that maybe we could do...we can't do the show for you, we don't have sets and lights, but maybe we could sing the songs from the show and tell you a little bit about how we did the story? And, this was Eric Moores, he goes, "Nah, there'll be nobody out here interested in anything like that." So I said, "Well you know what, maybe we'll just do it anyway." We contacted the churches and asked them to put it in their church bulletin. A free, little, drop-by-and-see-this [type of thing]. We're going to do it at seven o'clock. We got set up. We had to pick up the key from Eric Moores's house, and he said again, "No girl, they won't be interested in that." So we got set up, and we had the doors closed doing a sound check, and I remembering opening the door at five to seven, and there were about 50 people out there.

They came in, sat down. We told them what we were about. Just when we were about to start, who came in but Eric Moores himself. The students sang the songs from it, and I narrated what the story was and explained how Solomon Strong was the storyteller. Afterwards, true to Newfoundlanders, it was: "Would you like a few sandwiches?" "Do you want to come up to the house for a cup of tea?" As I was talking to these older people, I was watching my students disappear. Some of the locals said, "We'll take you up to the swimming hole." Provided all the towels. Put them all in the back of an open truck. Half a mile away. No chaperones.

Elizabeth Burry: The first night we spent in Harry's Harbour.

Gary Follett: We all slept on the floor. The adults, including myself, my wife Susan, Elizabeth, Paul Lahey, Jim Power, [some others], and 16 or 18 students. I'd say about half the kids in the play went.

Jacinta Mackey-Graham: The next morning, it was heavy rain. Selby Knight said, "I don't know if you should go over there." Eric Moores said, "What do you want to be going over there for?" But we had said, "We're doing it."

Elizabeth Burry: And we took a boat the next morning to the island. It wasn't real warm. It was amazing to see the kids demonstrate such maturity. These are high school kids. They embraced it. And that weekend wouldn't have happened if it wasn't for Gary. We would have packed up and left.

Gary Follett: Going over on the boat was quite pleasant.

Emily Follett: All the dads went [first] and the dads' kids.

Gary Follett: It was a nice day. It was relatively calm. We were piled into this [40-ft] reconditioned pleasure boat, [operated by Selby Knight] a fellow from Grand Falls. When we got over to the island—over there there's no wharf—we had to row back and forth from this boat in a smaller boat. We had to row into the shore and get off on the beach and turn around—

Elizabeth Burry: —All the gear—

Gary Follett: We were quite a while at that because we did have a lot of gear, a lot of tents and tarps and stoves and fold-up tables—

Elizabeth Burry: —And all the kids, they had everything they owned.

Gary Follett: That's true enough. So that was a bit of a production. But these kids were all doers. It was no trouble to get them all helping.

Jacinta Mackey-Graham: No cellphones worked on the island. We did have a satellite phone because we had one girl with us who was a severe diabetic. Once we were out on that island, we were abandoned.

Gary Follett: Lucky for us it was a nice day. It was pretty sheltered. It was easy getting off the boat. There was no wind where we got off. So we got on the island and spent most of the day exploring the island. The kids went over to the two graveyards: the Catholic graveyard and the [Methodist] graveyard. [Eric Moores had come over to check on them, and he showed them where to find the headstones.] And Mr. Strong was in the [Methodist] graveyard. He was the storyteller. He was the ghost that came back and told the story to the campers. There's a monument on the island to Stephen Norris. I don't know if his body was never found but it's not there.

Jaakob Palasvirta: As a side note, in the show we did have a coffin, draped in the Union Jack.

Gary Follett: In the middle or early afternoon—

Elizabeth Burry: It started to drizzle. It got cold. The temperature dropped. It started to get a little bit miserable.

Gary Follett: I had a big, huge, long, old tarp, so we set that tarp up over everything and got our tables underneath the tarp and cooked up lunch. And spent the day telling stories, and we were doing this [game], a parent would give a clue about something they did when they were a youngster, and the other kids would have to try and figure out which parent it was.

Jacinta Mackey-Graham: We sat under tarps for most of the day; what was amazing about that was without cellphones and without iPods. We had to make up games. We found out a lot about each other.

Elizabeth Burry: Why we started doing that was because we were getting wet and cold. And at this point, we were all starting to think, should we stay? [Gary] had to take a couple of kids down to a cabin to get dry. Gary found an old cabin.

Gary Follett: It was on the way over to the second graveyard. Myself and Dave and Jim and Paul, we took a bunch of these kids and went over to this cabin. We didn't have to break it open. The door was not locked. We lit a fire in there, and they came over and dried out and got warm again.

Jacinta Mackey-Graham: Probably about six o'clock the weather abated.

Gary Follett: The rain stopped. Because then we went and we picked mussels, and [Elizabeth] had bought corn from Ontario.

Elizabeth Burry: I got a case of peaches and cream corn shipped down from my girlfriend in Ontario.

Gary Follett: We boiled the mussels and cooked the corn up.

Elizabeth Burry: It was great.

Gary Follett: Yeah it was. We had an outside fire going. We spent the night around the fire. The kids were doing the ghost story stuff. Something that I realized—I think I was the only one there that didn't believe in ghosts.

There's two moments that I really remember. One was Elizabeth plays the trumpet.

Jacinta Mackey-Graham: Our plan was to do a ceremony at Stephen Norris's tombstone. It was right on the Norris property because there was no set Catholic graveyard there. It was up behind where the Norris house had been.

Gary Follett: The whole idea was we were going to go up to the monument for Stephen Norris. The kids had brought over some soil with them and some poppy seeds.

Jacinta Mackey-Graham : We bought our torches. We had a simple ceremony. We planted poppies and had a very short prayer for him. And we did the "Ode to Newfoundland."

Gary Follett: So they went up, and they put the soil down in front of the monument, and they set these seeds, a very sombre moment, and now it has just come on dark, and the mist is sort of like rolling in almost like a fog: calm, dead still, absolutely dead still. And off in the woods—and I get goose bumps now thinking about it, tell you the truth—off in the woods comes this trumpet playing—

Elizabeth Burry: "Last Post." I was in the woods being eaten alive.

Gary Follett: She couldn't have timed it any better. It was eerie.

Elizabeth Burry: [Jacinta] said at a certain time, seven or whatever, I was to start to play. We synchronized our watches. [My son Nick] said the faces…

Jacinta Mackey-Graham: I guess I should have told the students about that because it scared them right out of their wits. I just thought it would be very ethereal, that it wasn't directly there, that it would sound very haunting. Well, haunting would be the word, but not in the way that it was expected.

Gary Follett: That was a real moment. It was really emotional. I don't know what other way to describe it.

Jacinta Mackey-Graham: When we came down from the hill, we lit a bonfire. We asked everybody to bring something [to perform]. People sang Newfoundland songs or people did recitations, and we eventually got into ghost stories. Some of them stayed in tents and the rest of us in the cabin because our tarps, which were meant to go under the tents, had to go above because of the rain.

Gary Follett: But now remember I said it got really calm and still. Now we go back and we light an outside fire, and we're sitting around the fire telling stories.

Elizabeth Burry: And it was nice, beautiful then. It cleared right off.

Gary Follett: The sky got right clear. It was a little cool. We were wrapped up in whatever we had with us.

Elizabeth Burry: We had a great time singing and telling stories.

Gary Follett: Then it came time to go to bed, to bunk down for the night. All the rain's gone, and it had been dead calm. At the end of the island where we were, the bay goes in. You could really hear your echo. It was a little spooky. So we all start to bunk down. Right out of nowhere comes this huge wind—

Emily Follett: There was a big, big, big gust of wind in the middle, just one big gust, and all the tents and the table blew over.

Jacinta Mackey-Graham: The tents blew down in the night—

Elizabeth Burry: Just like that—

Gary Follett: We were exposed, in the teeth of it. We had a big huge monstrous tarp that was now a big huge monstrous sail, so the first thing we had to do was get that down—everyone in their pyjamas. Got the tarp down and got everything secured—the tents. You had almost to get in the tents so they wouldn't blow away—

Elizabeth Burry: It was unreal. It came like a train.

Gary Follett: The kids say, "Solomon Strong didn't mind us visiting his island, but he didn't like the fact that we stayed there." And then as quickly as it started, it stopped.

Elizabeth Burry: And we had a great night. But that was the weirdest, spookiest thing ever.

Jacinta Mackey-Graham: The next morning was absolutely beautiful.

"When Stephen Norris left Three Arms Island, that string that was cut was the heart of it all. Once it was set in motion, things happened pretty quickly after that...James Norris never really accepted Stephen's choice to go to war. So he never accepted that Stephen had died in the war... [It] caused his heart to break...with Stephen and James gone there was no one to run the business and eventually the fleet was sold off and the doors closed."
— Solomon Strong, *A Call to Arms*

Sarah Loveys: Being there on the island...I saw the gravesite of Mary Norris.[81] That was really, really something. And to have been in Harry's Harbour the evening before—we put on a show, selections from the show, as a thank you—and talking to the locals and getting their little stories about things that they knew about Three Arms Island, the people of Three Arms Island. They said it was haunted. By the spirits of the island. Just being there on the island, there's nothing there, besides this graveyard, and a beaten down shack that some of us camped in, The Hotel Three Arms—

Jaakob Palasvirta: And the remains of a boat on the shore.

Gary Follett: An old derelict boat. Well, there was remnants of something there, perhaps of a boat.

Jacinta Mackey-Graham: I didn't want to take things from the island. In our concept for the stage sets, for the wharf, we told the story of how Stephen's boat was docked there, and that I think we found the research [supporting] that. The father was so broken hearted, he wouldn't allow the boat to be sold or to be brought up on the land, and it stayed there moored to the Norris wharf until it rotted. Eric Moores said, "Oh yes, that was here for years. It rotted here on the beach."

---

[81] Mary Norris, born 1856 – died 1950 in Montreal.

Alicia Eaton (daughter of Bernard Norris, and niece of Stephen Norris): Eric Moores said Stephen had a boat, and it was never touched after, and it disintegrated. It was very sad.

Jacinta Mackey-Graham: I came across these nails, and Eric Moores said, "Yes my dear, most possibly they're from [Stephen Norris's boat, *The You and I*]."

Alicia Eaton: It just killed grandpa, and Uncle John died very close to that, after, so there was nothing in place, so everything had to be re-organized. There were only two brothers left. Dad and Uncle 'Brose. They picked up the bits.

Jacinta Mackey-Graham: When we wrote the story, we were so short on time, some of the naysayers in the class said, "We're not going to finish it!" And I said, "We started this, and we will finish this. We owe this to Stephen Norris's family." But we didn't know there was any of his family alive.

John Wheeler: Gonzaga put on the show. Then Heather Barrett at CBC did one piece on *Weekend AM*. That's how I learned about the play. It was like the hair raising on the back of your neck.

Jacinta Mackey-Graham: We did the show in the middle of May. We just did the Friday and Saturday night. In September, there was a piece [rebroadcast] on *Weekend AM*, and on Monday morning there was a phone call to Gonzaga. The secretary said, "There's a woman on the phone wants to speak to you. She's calling from Pasadena." I could tell it was an older lady. And she said, "Are you the lady who just directed a show about Stephen Norris?" I said, "Yes, I am." She said, "Stephen Norris was my uncle."

John Wheeler: The same morning I heard it, Alicia Eaton heard it out in Pasadena. It had the same effect for her.

Alicia Eaton: It was a Saturday morning, and I was in my kitchen in Pasadena. I heard someone say, "Stephen Norris.

I'm playing the part of Stephen Norris." I did get Jacinta's name, so I called her.

Jacinta Mackey-Graham: We were telling this story not knowing that there were any people alive. We just wanted to tell the story because it was interesting. She said, "I was Alicia Norris. I'm Alicia Eaton."

John Wheeler: Alicia would be my mom's first cousin. She got in contact with Jacinta, and I got in contact with Jacinta. And then we brought information together.

Jacinta Mackey-Graham: John Wheeler, from Torbay, contacted me and said, "That's my family. He would be a great-uncle of mine."

Alicia Eaton: The operetta had already been done, but I said, "I've got to see it."

Jacinta Mackey-Graham: I felt like we should do the show again, for the family.

So, Gonzaga mounted an encore presentation of A Call to Arms *in May 2005. The theatre was packed.*

John Wheeler: The second show, then, a lot of my cousins and Alicia were attendants for the second show, and that was very touching, for sure. Very emotional, very emotional. It was bringing the story life.

Jacinta Mackey-Graham: I didn't know this at the time, but this was a very fractured family situation. [The defunct business, remarriages, and other issues had left family lines estranged.] We sat them all together. They hadn't spoken in decades. It was kind of forced upon them. But good things come out of bad. It was a way of reconnecting.

Alicia Eaton: I met John again. We'd had no contact for a long time; there was always a split in the family. We were the East End Norrises, and they were the West End Norrises.

And that was nice to meet them all. I didn't know any of the cousins.

In fact, there was a family member there none of them had known about: Ambrose Norris's grand-daughter.[82]

Alicia Eaton: [The play] was fantastic. I met the cast: they were wonderful. I was the only one left of that generation. I'm a great-grandmother. I didn't think I'd get there, but I did.

It was a great feeling to realize it had been done. And then, of course, Three Arms itself, it's not even on the map now. When Jacinta took them out to the island, she said it was amazing. I know what she means. It is a beautiful spot I must say.

Jacinta Mackey-Graham: Probably about [2010] I was contacted by a guy named Stephen Norris who teaches at the University of Alberta. His grandfather would have been Stephen's cousin. I said, "You need to contact John Wheeler and get on the family tree. Everybody else is!"

Wheeler's extensive and meticulous Norris family tree includes family names, marriages, offspring, and homes located from Tilting, Fogo, to Ashland, Kentucky. And these lines would be drawn together as the momentum of the play now created a second excursion to Three Arms.

John Wheeler: We had been talking, as a family, of getting together and going to Three Arms. Going to the show was sort of the impetus. In August 2008, 32 or 33 of us [went], all some

---

[82] Ambrose Norris died in 1938 when he was knocked overboard from his ship, *The Granite*, off Catalina and en route for Conche. He was married, but he and his wife had no children. However, it transpired that he had fathered a child, in Conche, and that family line continues.

relation to the Norrises, from as far afield as New York and [Calgary]. Stephen Norris teaches at the University of Alberta. I'd never met him before, and now we've developed a friendship. We got together and arranged a weekend in Springdale, and for Selby Knight to take us over for Three Arms. We went over just for the day. Again, [it was] incredibly emotional. My first cousin, Brian Dunne, he is a priest. Now he is the bishop of Antigonish. Brian celebrated mass.

Still much taken with Stephen Norris's story, Wheeler also retraced part of the Regiment's journey in France.

John Wheeler: In 2010, we made the trip to Northern France and followed the Trail of the Caribou. We travelled to Gueudecourt. You could see the exact ground on which the battle was fought and still [find] evidence of some of the trenches. Just to be there and to see the minutiae of ground over which they were fighting...You could throw a rock across the lines.

Meanwhile, still at Gonzaga, Mackey-Graham was hearing from more and more people related to Stephen Norris's story.

Jacinta Mackey-Graham: This out-of-the-blue phone call came from this woman, [her last name was] Jesseau, in Grand Falls, who had heard something of this story. She was speaking to her grandmother, whom she called "Mom"; her grandmother was in Carmelite House, which used to be the old convent in Grand Falls [and is now an old age home]. This lady had a trunk, and the granddaughter was going through the trunk—"Mom, what's this?" and "Mom, what's that?"—and she took out a tin picture of a guy in uniform and said, "Now, Mom, who's that? That's not granddad." And [her grandmother] said, "No, that was the love of my life, Stephen Norris." So [the granddaughter] found a way to get in touch with me, and I said, "Oh my goodness, in our writing of the play we created a romantic interest, took licence with that for drama purposes, and called her Sophie." We went through old-fashioned names, and thought, "OK, Sophie sounds like a nice, old-fashioned name."

But her name was Johannah Alyward. And she was from Fortune Harbour and educated at Littledale and got her teacher certificate and had her first teaching job in Conche. Stephen Norris was running the company for his father that summer in Conche. This was after he had come from St. Bon's and didn't want to work in the family business. He wanted to be a doctor, and the father was insisting, "No, I need you to run this family business." So Stephen Norris met Johannah. They dated all summer, and then he said he was going overseas. And she was really, really upset with him for leaving, but he said, "I won't be gone long." That's what we wrote. That's what scary. That's what the echoes of this... There are no [six] degrees of separation in Newfoundland.

Every time I think this story is over another page turns.

Even as the short arc of Stephen Norris's life continues on this trajectory, touching more and more people, the students of Gonzaga Theatre Arts 3200, their teacher, and their parents are left with their own thoughts about the Great War.

Gary Follett: It's a funny thing, you know. Whatever it was about, that play and that weekend, to say that it was life-changing is probably a bit of an overstatement, but I'll tell you what: it definitely had an effect on both my life and Emily's life, my daughter. She was Sophie in the play. She was Stephen Norris's girlfriend in the play. And whatever it was about it, Emily drew me into it, and I have no ability to write a book, but I thought about it. What really came out in my mind was the senseless loss of life. And the senseless loss of a generation. And I said many times if I could write a book, I would write a book, and, it's not really a new idea, the book would start off with a bullet coming out of a gun, heading for Stephen Norris, to kill him. And in the time it took that bullet to get from the gun to Stephen Norris, the other life would come out, the life he would have had. Maybe he would have gone on to become some famous something or other, I don't know. It would end with the bullet hitting him. I tell you that's the kind of thoughts...I'm not one of these soft, touchy feely arts types....

JOHANNAH (NÉE ALYWARD) MCHUGH (C. 1915)

Elizabeth Burry: He's a man's man.

Gary Follett: That play brought out stuff like that in me, for whatever reason. The whole story.

Elizabeth Burry: For me, I felt closer [to WWI]. It made it more real. It made me put a face and a person to the event. I didn't have anybody in my family in any war other then the Korean War, my uncle, and he came back alive. [Stephen Norris and the Norris family] was my war family, and it gave me a connection to something we should all be connected to.

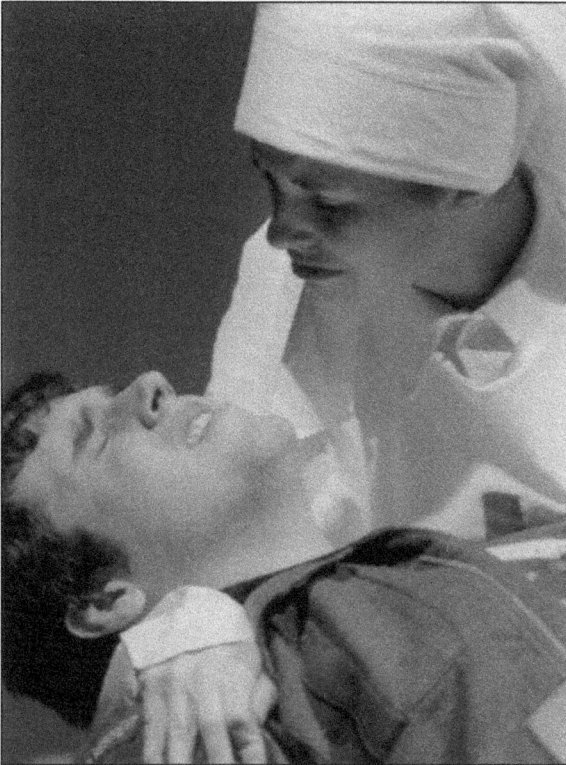

JOSH BOURDEN AS STEPHEN NORRIS AND JOANNA PARSONS as field nurse Emma Knight in the Gonzaga High School Production of *A Call to Arms*.

Jaakob Palasvirta: Now I feel I have an intimate understanding, that I can relate. I have an image of what the soldier's life was like. I know something about what women did if they wanted to go over, and I have a picture in my head of what life might have been like for the people in this community. All kinds of things like that. Whenever I hear about the First World War, it's not just facts. I can spin an image, and I have a set of feelings and an empathy.

Sarah Loveys: I don't actually know how to say it, but, having done this show and seen your friends, we were a close knit group, to see Josh [Bourden] play a role like [Stephen Norris], it put a face to the name.

Jaakob Palasvirta: It was very operatic.

Sarah Loveys: It was very moving. It made it more personal. It made it more real. That's what I took from it. And in the future and even now thinking back on all the lives that were lost, the children's lives, it makes you wonder: What's changed? Really nothing's changed. Back then people fought face to face. Whereas now you press a button. Can you put a face to those names? It is so important to bring attention to these stories. Sometimes they go untold. That's what we did.

Jacinta Mackey-Graham: We, as Newfoundlanders, have to tell our story because that's how we keep our history alive.

Sarah Loveys & Jaakob Palasvirta: Because their story is told to you, their story will live on.

Jaakob Palasvirta: That's the final words in the song at the end ["Their Story"]. But you might change it to something like, because their story is told to you, a story will live on. Because that's the best we can do.

Sarah Loveys: Because so much has come from it.

Jaakob Palasvirta: And we're part of the story now.

Jacinta Mackey-Graham: One degree of separation, that's

how this story has unfolded. That's what made this piece so lovely, so artistic, aside from the resonance.

Emily Follett: I have a huge connection to the First World War, and I also have a big sense of where I'm from and who my family is, and being away was impossible, and now I'm back.[83]

John Wheeler: The impact that the First World War has had is incredible. This was the cream of Newfoundlanders. All these young men, if they had not gone to war or if they had come back, would have been the leaders of an independent Newfoundland in the 1940s. The vacuum that that created certainly had an impact on history. And the way Newfoundland became a province, really. Who knows?

Jacinta Mackey-Graham: When you're teaching, it's incumbent upon you to do something for November 11th every year. You kind of do it somewhat out of duty, out of respect, but not always with anything of a connection because I didn't have any family members that I know of that were so adversely connected with it. I think this story and the effect that it had on the family beyond the battlefield, it makes you realize how profoundly affected Newfoundlanders were. How much families gave. I think that will forever colour the way I feel about anything to do with war.

John Wheeler: And it's not just Steve. He was one of hundreds. I'm sure he would have been a strong leader, just

---

[83]   Additionally, Palasvirta, Loveys, and Follett have all pursued careers as professional musicians. Palasvirta has a Master's degree in voice from McGill and in 2012 was hired as the organist at St. Andrew's Presbyterian Church (The Kirk) in St. John's. Loveys attended the MUN School of Music and Dalhousie Faculty of Music and studied voice in London at Guildhall. Follett has a BA in Music Education from MUN, and a Master's in Musical Theatre from the University of Western Ontario. They all cite the experience of working on *A Call to Arms* as a major influence, and credit Mackey-Graham "a lot."

from his personality. Just from what we know. He was the son of a business man, he had the business sense, it was a very thriving business, and it was snuffed out. It probably did contribute to the demise of the community. I don't think it had quite as much of an impact as the play made out because this was happening everywhere around the coast of Newfoundland at the time, not just Three Arms. There was resettlement before the resettlement of the 1960s. These communities, on islands particularly, a lot of people were moving to the mainland part just for convenience.

Gary Follett: It made me mad. At the administration that sucked all these poor little youngsters into going over and standing up in front of a bullet. It adds to my own personal feelings that when you're dead you're dead. There is no life after. I really don't believe in ghosts. We laugh sometimes at the [cliché of the] Arabs who talk about when you die you go to heaven and have seven virgins waiting for you, but we're actually no different. "There's this greater place that you're going to so it's sort of OK that you're going to die." In my case, it made me mad. I look at these poor youngsters who died, in a lot of cases, absolutely horrible deaths, and what went with them was a tremendous amount of future. Of ability, of new generations.

Elizabeth Burry: It robbed them of their contribution. It robbed that era of their contribution.

Gary Follett: And who knows what a different Newfoundland it would be? If you don't believe in your life after death then you believe in your responsibility to stay alive and do whatever you can do in the meantime. This whole event got me thinking about that. This play, this little school play....

Alicia Eaton: It was nice to sort of put an ending to it. It just came out of the blue. Almost like somebody telling you, "Go—and do— and look."

SOURCES

❀

Adelphian (1905).

———— 14:1 (1917).

Beckett, Ian F. *The Great War 1914-1918*. 2nd ed. Harlow: Pearson Education Limited, 2007.

Brooke, Rupert. *Rupert Brooke: The Collected Poems*. London: Sidgwick & Jackson, 1987.

Burry, Elizabeth. Interview with the author. March 19, 2012.

Cave, Joy B. *What Became of Corporal Pittman?* St. John's: Breakwater Books, 1976.

Cramm, Richard. *The First Five Hundred, Being a historical sketch of the military operations of the Royal Newfoundland Regiment in Gallipoli and on the Western Front during the Great War (1914-1918)*. New York: C. F. Williams, 1921.

Christie, Norm. *For King & Empire: The Newfoundlanders in the Great War 1916-1918*. Ottawa: CEF Books, 2003.

Eaton, Alicia. Interview with the author. May 14, 2012.

The Encyclopedia of Newfoundland and Labrador. St. John's: Harry Cuff Publications Ltd., 1994.

Facey-Crowther, David R., ed. *Better Than the Best: The Story of Royal Newfoundland Regiment 1795-1995*. The Royal Newfoundland Regiment Advisory Council, 1995.

Facey-Crowther, David R, ed. *Lieutenant Owen William Steele of the Newfoundland Regiment, Diary and Letters*. Montreal: McGill-Queen's University Press, 2002.

Facey-Crowther, David R. "The Soldier's Tale: Newfoundland Soldiers' Accounts of The Great War." Talk presented to the Newfoundland Genealogical Society, November 23, 1999.

Facey-Crowther, David R. "War and Remembrance: Soldiers' Diaries, Letters and Memories of The Great War." Talk presented to the Newfoundland Museum, November 14, 1999.

Fewster, Kevin, Veciji Başarm, and Hatice Hürmüz Başarm. *Gallipoli: The Turkish Story*. Crows Nest, Australia: Allen and Unwin, 2003.

Firstworldwar.com. "Weapons of War." Last modified August 22, 2009. http://www.firstworldwar.com/weaponry/gas.htm

Follett, Emily. Interview with the author. April 23, 2012.

Follett, Gary. Interview with the author. March 19, 2012.

Gilbert, Wm. "NFLD Regiment: Its Volunteer Patterns, Aug. 1914 to July 17, 1917." Unpublished paper, Memorial University, 1980.

The Guardian, "The Comedy of War." Last modified November 10, 2008. http://www.guardian.co.uk/world/2008/nov/10/first-world-war-humour-wipers-times

Gonzaga Theatre Arts Class. *A Call to Arms*. Theatrical Production. St. John's, 2004.

Hibbs, Richard, ed. *Who's Who in and from Newfoundland*, 1927. St. John's: 1927.

Lind, Francis T. *The Letters of Mayo Lind, Newfoundland's Unofficial War Correspondent 1914-1916*. St. John's: Robinson & Co., Limited, 1919; St. John's: Creative Book Publishing, 2001.

Loveys, Sarah. Interview with the author. April 12, 2012.

Macfarlane, David. *The Danger Tree: Memory, War, and the Search for a Family's Past*. Toronto: Macfarlane Walter & Ross, 1991.

Mackey-Graham, Jacinta. Interview with the author. April 23, 2012.

Martin, Chris. "'The Right Course, The Best Course, The Only Course': Voluntary Recruitment in the Newfoundland Regiment 1914-1918." Unpublished paper, Memorial University, 2008.

Nangle, Captain Rev. Thomas. *The Trail of the Caribou*. St. John's: 1918.

"New Lieutenants–Newfoundland Regiment," *Newfoundland Quarterly* 15.3 (1916): 3-5.

Nicholson, Gerald W. L. *The Fighting Newfoundlander: A History of The Royal Newfoundland Regiment.* Montreal: McGill-Queen's University Press, 2006.

O'Brien, Michael (Assistant Professor, Department of History, Memorial University). Interview with the author. April 2, 2012.

Owen, Wilfred. *Wilfred Owen: The War Poems.* Edited by Jon Stallworthy. London: Chatto & Windus, 1994.

Palasvirta, Jaakob. Interview with the author. April 12 and 23, 2012.

"Reveille," *Newfoundland Quarterly* 104.1 (2011).

Riggs, Bert (Archivist, QEII Library Archives and Special Collections, Memorial University). Interview with the author. April 16, 2012.

Skanes, Roy. "A History of Three Arms Island." Unpublished Paper, Memorial University, 1978.

Wheeler, John, and Brenda Wheeler. Interview with the author. May 9, 2012.

Wheeler, John. Private collection.

❀

Photographs on pages 6, 16, 23, 36, 37, 45, 46, 60 and 77
courtesy of John Wheeler.

Photographs on pages 85, 89, 107 and 108
courtesy of Jacinta Mackey-Graham.

❀

**Special thanks to Dr. Robert Finley and the
class of English 4913, Winter 2012.
And a very special thank you to Iain McCurdy.**

JOAN SULLIVAN is the editor of the *Newfoundland Quarterly*. As a freelance journalist, her interviews, reviews, and commentary have appeared in *The Telegram*, *The Globe and Mail*, and on CBC Radio's *Tapestry*.

A playwright, director, and actor, Sullivan has most recently appeared as guest director at the Grand Bank Regional Theatre Festival and in cahoots with the Document Theatre Collective in St. John's.

www.ingramcontent.com/pod-product-compliance
Lightning Source LLC
Chambersburg PA
CBHW021406090426
42742CB00009B/1030